T0384921

An Analysis of

Gilbert Ryle's

The Concept of Mind

Michael O'Sullivan

Published by Macat International Ltd
24:13 Coda Centre, 189 Munster Road, London SW6 6AW.

Distributed exclusively by Routledge
2 Park Square, Milton Park, Abingdon, Oxon OX14 4RN
711 Third Avenue, New York, NY 10017, USA

Routledge is an imprint of the Taylor & Francis Group, an informa business

Copyright © 2017 by Macat International Ltd
Macat International has asserted its right under the Copyright, Designs and Patents Act
1988 to be identified as the copyright holder of this work.

www.macat.com
info@macat.com

Cataloguing in Publication Data
A catalogue record for this book is available from the British Library.
Library of Congress Cataloguing-in-Publication Data is available upon request.
Cover illustration: Etienne Gilfillan

ISBN 978-1-912303-13-7 (hardback)
ISBN 978-1-912127-13-9 (paperback)
ISBN 978-1-912282-01-2 (e-book)

Notice

CONTENTS

THE MACAT LIBRARY

The Macat Library is a series of unique academic explorations of seminal works in the humanities and social sciences – books and papers that have had a significant and widely recognised impact on their disciplines. It has been created to serve as much more than just a summary of what lies between the covers of a great book. It illuminates and explores the influences on, ideas of, and impact of that book. Our goal is to offer a learning resource that encourages critical thinking and fosters a better, deeper understanding of important ideas.

Each publication is divided into three Sections: Influences, Ideas, and Impact. Each Section has four Modules. These explore every important facet of the work, and the responses to it.

This Section-Module structure makes a Macat Library book easy to use, but it has another important feature. Because each Macat book is written to the same format, it is possible (and encouraged!) to cross-reference multiple Macat books along the same lines of inquiry or research. This allows the reader to open up interesting interdisciplinary pathways.

To further aid your reading, lists of glossary terms and people mentioned are included at the end of this book (these are indicated by an asterisk [*] throughout) – as well as a list of works cited.

Macat has worked with the University of Cambridge to identify the elements of critical thinking and understand the ways in which six different skills combine to enable effective thinking.
Three allow us to fully understand a problem; three more give us the tools to solve it. Together, these six skills make up the **PACIER** model of critical thinking. They are:

ANALYSIS – understanding how an argument is built
EVALUATION – exploring the strengths and weaknesses of an argument
INTERPRETATION – understanding issues of meaning

CREATIVE THINKING – coming up with new ideas and fresh connections
PROBLEM-SOLVING – producing strong solutions
REASONING – creating strong arguments

To find out more, visit **WWW.MACAT.COM.**

CRITICAL THINKING AND *THE CONCEPT OF MIND*

Primary critical thinking skill: REASONING
Secondary critical thinking skill: INTERPRETATION

Gilbert Ryle's 1949 *The Concept of Mind* is now famous above all as the origin of the phrase "the ghost in the machine" – a phrase Ryle used to attack the popular idea that our bodies and minds are separate. His own position was that mental acts are not at all distinct from bodily actions. Indeed, they are the same thing, merely described in different ways – and if one cuts through the confusing language of the old philosophical debates, he suggests, that becomes clear.

While, in many ways, modern philosophers of mind have moved on from or discarded Ryle's actual arguments, *The Concept of Mind* remains a classic example of two central critical thinking skills: interpretation and reasoning. Ryle was what is known as an "ordinary language" philosopher – a school who considered many philosophical problems to exist purely because of philosophical language. He therefore considered his task as a philosopher to be one of cutting through confusing language, and clarifying matters – exemplifying the critical thinking skill of interpretation at its best. Rather than adding to philosophical knowledge as such, moreover, he saw his role as one of mapping it – giving it what he called a "logical geography." As such, *The Concept of Mind* is also all about reasoning: laying out, organizing, and systematizing clear arguments.

ABOUT THE AUTHOR OF THE ORIGINAL WORK

Born in the English town of Brighton in 1900, philosopher **Gilbert Ryle** spent all of his academic life at the University of Oxford, first studying Latin and Greek, and then lecturing in philosophy. He worked with British military intelligence during World War II, before returning to philosophical matters, primarily exploring the relationship between mind and body. This work was best encapsulated in his 1949 book, *The Concept of Mind*. He also edited the philosophical journal *Mind* between the years of 1947 and 1971. Ryle died in 1976 after a short retirement.

ABOUT THE AUTHOR OF THE ANALYSIS

Dr Michael O'Sullivan is a tutor in the Department of Philosophy, King's College London. He is the editor of *Wittgenstein and Perception*.

ABOUT MACAT

GREAT WORKS FOR CRITICAL THINKING

Macat is focused on making the ideas of the world's great thinkers accessible and comprehensible to everybody, everywhere, in ways that promote the development of enhanced critical thinking skills.

It works with leading academics from the world's top universities to produce new analyses that focus on the ideas and the impact of the most influential works ever written across a wide variety of academic disciplines. Each of the works that sit at the heart of its growing library is an enduring example of great thinking. But by setting them in context – and looking at the influences that shaped their authors, as well as the responses they provoked – Macat encourages readers to look at these classics and game-changers with fresh eyes. Readers learn to think, engage and challenge their ideas, rather than simply accepting them.

'Macat offers an amazing first-of-its-kind tool for interdisciplinary learning and research. Its focus on works that transformed their disciplines and its rigorous approach, drawing on the world's leading experts and educational institutions, opens up a world-class education to anyone.'

Andreas Schleicher
Director for Education and Skills, Organisation for Economic
Co-operation and Development

'Macat is taking on some of the major challenges in university education … They have drawn together a strong team of active academics who are producing teaching materials that are novel in the breadth of their approach.'

Prof Lord Broers,
former Vice-Chancellor of the University of Cambridge

'The Macat vision is exceptionally exciting. It focuses upon new modes of learning which analyse and explain seminal texts which have profoundly influenced world thinking and so social and economic development. It promotes the kind of critical thinking which is essential for any society and economy.
This is the learning of the future.'

Rt Hon Charles Clarke, former UK Secretary of State for Education

'The Macat analyses provide immediate access to the critical conversation surrounding the books that have shaped their respective discipline, which will make them an invaluable resource to all of those, students and teachers, working in the field.'

Professor William Tronzo, University of California at San Diego

WAYS IN TO THE TEXT

KEY POINTS

- Gilbert Ryle (1900–1976) was a leading British philosopher.
- *The Concept of Mind* seeks to clarify the nature of the human mind and its relation to the body.
- The book is an influential attack on the idea that the mind and the body are distinct entities.

Who Was Gilbert Ryle?

Gilbert Ryle was born in Brighton, England, in 1900. He spent all his academic life at the University of Oxford, first as a student of Greek and Latin, and then as a lecturer in philosophy. He worked in British military intelligence during World War II.* After the war he became one of the most famous and influential British philosophers, dying in 1976.

The Concept of Mind, published in 1949, is Ryle's first and most important book. In it he explains his view of philosophical method—that is, the way he approaches philosophical problems—and then applies that method to a major philosophical problem. The problem he tackles is the relationship between mind and body.

The book had a huge influence on the way we think about the mind. Ryle both attacked traditional views of the mind and also put forward his own approach, which was as controversial as it was important.

The Concept of Mind is still widely read and popular with both students and the general public. But Ryle's reputation among philosophers has now declined. Many of them doubt that Ryle's method is the correct one, and his alternative view of the mind is not popular today. It is often considered to be at odds with contemporary science.

What Does *The Concept of Mind* Say?

We often think of the mind as being separate from the body. A human being, we believe, is made up of two distinct parts: a mind and a body. This view is known as dualism.* Dualists think of the mind as a non-physical entity that does not take up any space, but that must affect the body. When I decide to move my arm, for example, something happens in my mind that causes my arm to move.

But dualism causes problems. If the mind does not exist in space, how can it affect the body? And if the mind is not anywhere in space, it cannot be observed. How, then, do we come to know anything about the mind? Dualists often thought that a person can have direct knowledge of their own mind, but no direct knowledge of others' minds.

Ryle thinks dualism is a mistake. He calls the dualist view of the mind "the ghost in the machine," saying that dualists think of the body as a machine and of the mind as a ghost that inhabits it. Instead, he argues that the mind and the body are not distinct entities. Rather, they are simply different ways of describing a human being. When we say that someone is intelligent, for example, or lazy, we are not describing something inside them that is separate from their bodies. We are describing their behavior and how they are likely to behave.

I gain my knowledge of minds by observing and understanding behavior. This is true of my own mind as well as of other people's minds. How do I realize that I am bored, for example? I find myself yawning and fidgeting. This is roughly the same way that I find out that other people are bored.

Ryle thinks that dualism arises from confusion about concepts.* In philosophy, concepts are understood to be general ideas, or categories, that we have to help us understand the world. We need to clarify our concepts, so that once we are clear that the concept of "mind" is not a concept of anything that is an actual object, we will no longer be tempted to accept dualism.

Dualism is no longer a popular view among philosophers and scientists, but it is still a very common view within the wider culture. Much of our common sense is based on it, for instance. We often think of a person as inhabiting their body, rather than actually *being* that body. Dualism is also connected to traditional religious views. Many religious people, for example, believe that a human being is made up of a body *and* a soul. They think that the soul will live on when the body dies. So Ryle's argument against dualism is still of relevance to many.

Ryle's own view of the mind connects mental states to behavior. This view has not been widely accepted. Today we often think of mental states as complex internal conditions of human beings—though we do not think that they have nothing to do with the physical. We actually think these mental states are closely related to the brain. In fact, some think that mental states are actually structures or networks in the brain. So Ryle's argument against dualism, as well as challenging more traditional views of the mind, challenges views that are held today.

Ryle also puts forward an idea about philosophy. Philosophy, he says, does not aim to acquire more knowledge about the world—that is the role of science. Instead, philosophy tries to clarify our view of the world and helps us to understand more clearly the knowledge we already have.

The Concept of Mind has also had a broader cultural impact. The phrase "the ghost in the machine" has become famous as a means of describing what the scientific view of the world ignores or leaves out.

Why Does *The Concept of Mind* Matter?

The Concept of Mind is a major contribution to the discipline of the philosophy of the mind. It deals with an old and important problem—namely, does the mind relate to the body? It gives an answer that is important to understand, even if you disagree with it, and Ryle's book has clearly influenced later thought about the mind.

The Concept of Mind is important to psychology as well as to philosophy and contributes to an important debate about psychological method. Psychologists sometimes think that their job is to study behavior, rather than the mind itself. This is because many people feel that behavior can be observed while the mind cannot. They say psychology as a science should only deal with what you can observe. This was a particularly popular view in the early twentieth century. Ryle clarifies the connections between mind and behavior and suggests that when one studies behavior, one is, in fact, studying the mind.

Ryle's method is as important as his conclusions. He carefully studies how we talk about the mind. He thinks that dualism comes from a misunderstanding of the *concept* of mind and that this misunderstanding can be removed by clarifying what we *mean* when we use words that refer to the mind.

The method of solving problems by examining language is an important one. Ryle thinks it is the only way to approach philosophical questions. A number of more recent philosophers, such as David Armstrong* and Timothy Williamson,* disagree with this. But even if taking a close look at language is not the only way to approach these philosophical questions, we can still learn things from Ryle's method.

Ryle gives us a new way of thinking about the mind. Previous philosophers tried to answer the question "How does the mind affect the body?" Ryle changed the question, asking, for example, "What do we mean when we say 'I slammed the door because I was angry'?" He suggests an alternative way of understanding such an explanation for an action. He claims that in such a case, we are not saying what *caused* the action—rather, we are describing the action as belonging to a certain pattern of behavior.

The Concept of Mind is enjoyable to read. It is well written and often funny. Ryle shows humor and imagination in his examples and illustrations, while making many interesting points about specific types of mental state. There are chapters on, for example, the will, imagination, perception, and emotion. He argues, for instance, that the word "emotion" has several different senses. It can mean a feeling, like a shudder of fear. Or it can mean a tendency to behave in particular ways, such as in anger. In each of these chapters Ryle is arguing for his general theory of the mind, but the remarks he makes about these topics are also interesting in their own right.

SECTION 1
INFLUENCES

MODULE 1
THE AUTHOR AND THE HISTORICAL CONTEXT

KEY POINTS

- *The Concept of Mind* is a significant work in the philosophy of mind, and it was influential in its attack on the dualist* idea that the mind is a separate entity from the body.

- Ryle was interested in new developments in philosophy and psychology, including those occurring in continental Europe.

- After World War II,* Ryle became one of the most famous and influential British philosophers of the twentieth century.

Why Read This Text?

The Concept of Mind was published in 1949. It is Gilbert Ryle's first and most important book, and it is widely considered a modern philosophical classic. It is also one of the relatively few products of modern academic philosophy to have had a major impact within other disciplines, as well as outside the university system.

The book is a work on the philosophy of the mind and applies revolutionary new methods to traditional philosophical problems about the subject. Its title implies something about these methods: Ryle approaches the problem as one involving clarifying concepts*—defining our notions about how we understand the world. He describes himself as drawing a map of our mental concepts—not only the concept of mind itself, but related concepts, such as will, thought, intellect, feeling, and sensation.

> ❝ Without our noticing it at the time, hustings words ending in 'ism' and 'ist' faded out of our use. In this and other ways we were outgrowing some then prevalent attitudes towards philosophical issues. We discovered that it was possible to be at once in earnest and happy. ❞
>
> Gilbert Ryle, "Autobiographical"

Ryle's book is an attack on dualism—that is, the view that the mind and the body are distinct entities that together make up a human being. This view has been important in the history of philosophy and of religion, and it is also commonly held by ordinary people today. It relates, for example, to the widely held idea that the soul survives the body. Ryle's attack on dualism has been influential, and it is partly because of him that it is rare for any philosopher or psychologist to defend dualism today.

However, the book doesn't just knock down old ideas—it adds new ones of its own. As well as attacking dualism, Ryle puts forward an important alternative view of the mind. He argues that the mind and the body are not different things but are, rather, different ways of talking about the same thing: the human being. When we talk about human beings in terms of their minds, we are for the most part describing their typical and likely behavior.

Ryle's original theory of the mind is far more controversial than his attack on dualism. Many philosophers and psychologists today think he ties the mind too closely to behavior. Noam Chomsky* and Jerry Fodor* are prominent examples of intellectuals who disagree with Ryle's theory. But some, such as Daniel Dennett,* still share his approach.

Author's Life

Gilbert Ryle was born in Brighton, England, in 1900, and he received a classical education both in school and as an undergraduate at

Oxford.[1] He eventually rebelled against philosophy's classical leaning at Oxford and also against the dominant philosophical voices of his youth. Yet he did so only after he had learned a lot about them. He went to Oxford as a student of classics, and after graduating, he became a lecturer in philosophy there, so he spent his entire academic life at Oxford.

Ryle was one of the earliest English readers and interpreters of the phenomenological* school of the German philosophers Edmund Husserl* and Martin Heidegger,* which focuses on the way the world appears to individuals. More importantly for his own work, though, he also studied the writings of the logical positivist* school based in Vienna, most crucially those of another German philosopher, Rudolf Carnap.* This was a movement in philosophy which held that science is the only important means of acquiring knowledge—and, indeed, that the only meaningful sentences you can speak or write are those which can be tested by observation. This is a very radical thesis because it rules out religious and artistic language as meaningless, since one cannot factually check sentences like "God is good" or "Beethoven was a great composer." Despite his conservative background, Ryle became an early advocate of and contributor to ideas that revolutionized the philosophical landscape both at Oxford and beyond.

Oxford academic life was interrupted by World War II, when Ryle and other young thinkers entered the military. Like many other academics, Ryle worked in military intelligence. By the time the war ended in 1945, many of the older academics had retired, and a younger generation took over. So what had been a revolutionary movement in philosophy before World War II became the establishment afterward.

By the time he wrote *The Concept of Mind*, Ryle had become Waynflete Professor of Metaphysical Philosophy at Oxford and editor of the prestigious philosophical journal *Mind*, so he was a very senior figure in Oxford in the field of philosophy.

Author's Background

Ryle received a thorough classical education, with an excellent grounding in Greek and Latin, both in language and in philosophy, but he was also very curious about new ideas. During the 1920s and 1930s, when Ryle's views were forming, many new ideas were coming from continental Europe, and Ryle eagerly absorbed them. He was in an excellent position to criticize traditional and contemporary philosophical ideas because he knew and thoroughly understood the ideas that he was criticizing.

Ryle was brought up in a non-religious household, and he was never tempted to practice any religion.[2] In fact, there is little explicit reference, in either a positive or a negative way, to religion in his writings. However, his lack of religious faith may have influenced his lack of sympathy for belief in dualism concerning the mind and body, as dualism has often been associated with the religious idea that human beings have souls that can survive the death of the body.

World War II represented a watershed for British academic philosophy. Academic life was interrupted by the war, and when the conflict ended a new generation of philosophers took over. Thinkers like Ryle, who had been seen as radical before the war, now became part of a new establishment. *The Concept of Mind* was written at a crucial point when new ideas, many of them derived from continental Europe, entered the mainstream.

NOTES

1   Gilbert Ryle, "Autobiographical," in *Ryle*, ed. Oscar P. Wood and George Pitcher (London: Macmillan, 1971).

2   Ryle, "Autobiographical," 1.

MODULE 2
ACADEMIC CONTEXT

KEY POINTS

- The philosophy of mind concerns the nature of mental states such as belief, perception, and emotion and their relationship with the body.

- The scientific worldview, as it had developed since the sixteenth century, seemed to leave no room for the human mind.

- Ryle used the tools of modern philosophy to investigate the question of what the mind is.

The Work in its Context

Gilbert Ryle's book *The Concept of Mind* addresses this question: what is the relationship between mind and body? This question has deep roots in philosophical tradition, and particularly in philosophy since the seventeenth century. The scientific revolution at that time transformed our understanding of the world, and a new question arose: how could the human mind fit into the world as understood by science?

During the seventeenth century, a view of nature known as mechanical philosophy* had become dominant. This mechanical view believed that nature can be explained by the regular behavior and interaction of the microscopic parts that everything is made up of. These microscopic parts influence each other by direct contact, and the result of their activity is the natural world that we observe.

Like the rest of nature, the human body came to be understood better by using the model of a mechanism. The body is part of the inter-related network of nature, but this left the mind in a somewhat

> ❝ The goal of the book was to quell ... confusions
> about mental events and entities, the confusions
> that had generated the centuries-old pendulum
> swing between Descartes' dualism* (paramechanical
> hypotheses) and Hobbes's materialism* (mechanical
> hypotheses), both sides correctly discerning the main
> flaws in the other, but doomed to reproducing them in
> mirror image. ❞
>
> Daniel Dennett, "Re-introducing *The Concept of Mind*"

unusual position outside this network. The mind seems to interact
with the body—for example, I decide to move my right arm, and as a
result, my right arm moves. But scientists would not include the mind
itself—with its thoughts, feelings, and consciousness—in the
mechanical models they constructed.

Some philosophers and scientists, such as Thomas Hobbes* and
Pierre Gassendi,* proposed mechanistic models of the mind, but these
approaches were widely resisted. Frequently they were viewed as
dangerous and anti-religious. But even those who, like René
Descartes,* did not object to them on moral grounds saw them as
unacceptably crude. These mechanistic models of the mind did not
seem to account for the sophistication and complexity of the human
mind.

Overview of the Field

The French philosopher René Descartes* attempted to solve the
problem of the relationship between mind and body by suggesting the
idea of a non-physical, non-spatial mind[1]—that is, something that
doesn't exist in or take up space. Mind and body then become distinct
substances with contrasting natures. By its nature, a body takes up
space, while the mind doesn't and is characterized by consciousness. In

this view, since the mind is not part of the physical world, it is not subject to the laws of nature as discovered by science. Instead, it operates according to principles of its own.

As Descartes' contemporaries recognized, his view creates a puzzle about how mind and body can interact causally: that is, if it is not part of the physical world, how can the mind affect the body, as it does when I decide to act and then move my body accordingly? Further contradicting Descartes, it also seems as though there can be causal influences in the opposite direction; for example, my sense organs are stimulated, and as a result a thought arises in my mind. But if the mind is non-spatial, as Descartes theorized, how can such causal interactions take place?

Descartes' followers attempted to solve the problem of mind–body causation. One of his fellow French philosophers, Nicolas Malebranche,* for example, speculated that God ensures a logical link between mental and physical events. When I make the decision to move my arm, he claimed, God ensures that a moment later my arm moves: I myself do not cause the rising of the arm directly. But such solutions to the puzzle came to seem scientifically unacceptable. Scientists needed to explain worldly events in terms of worldly causes, and they no longer appealed to God in their explanations of how the world operated.

Academic Influences
By the twentieth century it was widely assumed that the scientific worldview was broadly correct. Further, it was thought unacceptable for philosophers discussing the mind–body problem to solve it by suggesting that non-physical entities, though invisible, were causally responsible for our behavior. This belief was seen as particularly unacceptable for the very reason that such entities would be unobservable. In scientists' view, it was essential for them to base all theories on observations that can be verified.

Yet Ryle did not wish to lapse into a crude materialism* that would see the mind as simply a myth or illusion because it was not "matter." We are not making a mistake, Ryle thought, when we say that I lifted my arm because I decided to do so. We do in fact make such decisions, but dualism* arises from a misinterpretation of what they represent.

His plan was to use philosophical analysis and argument to clarify the problem that he believed arose from a misunderstanding of the nature of explanations about thought processes. When we say that people act in a certain way because they are angry or lazy, he argued, we are not pointing to a cause of the behavior. Rather, we are pointing to a pattern of behavior. In this Ryle was influenced by recent trends within philosophy that saw the clarification of concepts as its main task. In different ways, the logical positivists* and the Austrian philosopher Ludwig Wittgenstein* believed in this trend.

NOTES

1   René Descartes, *Meditations on First Philosophy*, trans. and ed. John Cottingham (Cambridge: Cambridge University Press, 1996), 50–62.

MODULE 3
THE PROBLEM

KEY POINTS

- The core question in *The Concept of Mind* is: how should we explain behavior? In other words, is human behavior caused by unobservable mental states?

- Dualists* hold that the mind is an unobservable entity that lies behind behavior and explains it. But to behaviorists,* mental states are nothing more than behavior itself.

- Ryle rejected dualism and advocated a new view of the mind. Commentators disagree on whether this view is a form of behaviorism.

Core Question

The core question of Gilbert Ryle's *The Concept of Mind* might be phrased as follows: how should we explain human behavior? Common sense, and much of the philosophical tradition, concludes that there is an unobservable mind that lies behind our behavior and causes it. Is this view—usually known as dualism*—acceptable?

A related question is this: how do we gain knowledge of our own mind and the minds of others? In the dualist view, after all, minds are unobservable. We therefore cannot come to know them in the same way that we come to know about people's behavior or other observable aspects of the natural world.

Dualists tend to suggest that there is a major difference between how I come to know my own mind and how I come to know the minds of others. I have access to my own mind, and therefore I can know with certainty what is occurring in it. But I have to make assumptions about other people's mental states on the basis of their

> **"** No one in his senses can in practice regard himself or his friends or enemies simply as ingenious machines produced by other machines, or can regard his arm-chair or his poker as being literally societies of spirits or thoughts in the mind of God. It must not be supposed that the men who maintain these theories, and believe that they believe them, are 'silly' people. Only very acute and learned men could have thought of anything so odd or defended anything so preposterous against the continual protests of common sense. **"**
>
> C. D. Broad, *The Mind and Its Place in Nature*

observable behavior. I cannot have certain knowledge of what is occurring in other people's minds, and indeed I cannot know whether they have minds at all.

These are philosophical questions about the nature of the mind. But they are also methodological questions for psychologists, who have dedicated themselves to studying the mind. Like other empirical* scientists, psychologists conduct their studies by observation. So what methods can they use to make discoveries about the mind?

The Participants

Broadly speaking, two different solutions had at different times been popular among psychologists. In the late nineteenth century, the introspectionism* of experimental psychologist Wilhelm Wundt* was dominant. This is the view that psychologists can and should work by observing their own mental states.

Later, behaviorism* became more popular. This comes in a number of forms. Methodological behaviorists,* such as the psychologist John Watson,* felt that because mental states cannot be observed in the laboratory, psychology should instead concentrate on overt bodily behavior, which *can* be observed. If psychologists are interested in studying anger, for example, they should regard it not as a feeling known only to the subject who is experiencing it, but rather as a range of observable behavior. Such behavior might include movements of the arms, for example, or speaking more loudly.

Within philosophy, a different view emerged—one sometimes called logical behaviorism.* This is the view that mental states are just patterns of behavior. To be angry is just to behave in an angry way. Logical behaviorists such as German philosopher Rudolf Carnap* were influenced by empiricism.* Such philosophers wanted to show that our concepts spring from observation. Since it is only behavior that can be observed, words like "anger" must mean a form of behavior.[1]

Behaviorism was at its height when Ryle was writing. But what had not yet emerged was a philosophically satisfactory approach to the relation between mental states and overt behavior. Ryle's book is essentially a response to this need.

The Contemporary Debate

Ryle makes few explicit references to other thinkers. There are no footnotes in *The Concept of Mind* and few, if any, citations of literature. He mentions the dualism of René Descartes* as his target. Yet his interest is not so much in the historical details of Descartes' position as in the dualist view that Ryle noticed was common and that is frequently associated with Descartes.

Ryle's solution to the problem of mind involves making a strong connection between mental states and behavior. Mental states are tendencies to behave in various ways. To be angry, for example, is to be disposed to act angrily. Many commentators have described Ryle as a behaviorist. Some of the earliest reviewers of the book, for example, connected his thesis with behaviorism, and it is still common in textbooks on the philosophy of mind to introduce Ryle as an example of a proponent of this.[2] But Ryle himself denied this.[3] He does not hold that only behavior exists and only behavior can be studied, and equally he does not hold that the mind itself cannot be studied. Rather, he argues that mental states are real and are exhibited in behavior.

NOTES

1   Rudolf Carnap, "Psychology in Physical Language," *Erkenntnis* 3 (1932/33): 107–42.

2   A. J. Ayer, "An Honest Ghost?" in *Ryle*, ed. Oscar P. Wood and George Pitcher (London: Macmillan, 1971), 53–74; Morris Weitz, "Ryle's Logical Behaviorism," *Journal of Philosophy* 48 (1951): 297–301. For a more recent identification of Ryle as behaviorist, see Peter Smith and O. R. Jones, *Philosophy of Mind: An Introduction* (Cambridge: Cambridge University Press, 1986), 144.

3   Gilbert Ryle, *The Concept of Mind* (London: Penguin, 2000), 308–11.

MODULE 4
THE AUTHOR'S CONTRIBUTION

KEY POINTS

- Ryle understood mental states in terms of dispositions to behave in a certain way. In this view, the mind is not a hidden mechanism that explains observable behavior, but neither does it consist merely of such behavior.

- Ryle saw his task as one of resolving conceptual confusions. He thought that dualism* arose from a conceptual confusion he called a "category mistake."*

- He applied new philosophical methods—partly learned from the logical positivists,* Ludwig Wittgenstein,* and others—to an old problem.

Author's Aims

In his intellectual autobiography, Gilbert Ryle describes *The Concept of Mind* as "a philosophical book written with a metaphilosophical purpose."[1] Metaphilosophy* is the study of philosophy itself, its aims, and its methods. Ryle wrote this autobiography to show how his ideas about the philosophical method could be applied fruitfully to a serious philosophical problem.

Ryle believed that philosophical problems arise from confusions about concepts. If we could reach a clear understanding of our concepts,* he argued, the problems that have plagued philosophers for so long should disappear. Ryle and other philosophers had long argued that such conceptual analysis was the proper method of philosophy. By the late 1940s, he had decided that the method should be demonstrated in practice by applying it to a major philosophical issue in order to check how effective it was. His first thought was to address the problem

> 66 This book offers what may with reservations be described as a theory of the mind. But it does not give new information about minds. We possess already a wealth of information about minds, information which is neither derived from, nor upset by, the arguments of philosophers. The philosophical arguments which constitute this book are intended not to increase what we know about minds, but to rectify the logical geography of the knowledge which we already possess. 99

Gilbert Ryle, *The Concept of Mind*

of free will, but he then settled on the mind–body problem—that is, on how the mind and body are related.

In part, Ryle was applying new views in the field of logic* that had been developed earlier in the century. The revolution began at Cambridge University with the work of the philosophers Bertrand Russell* and Ludwig Wittgenstein,* and it was continued in Vienna by the logical positivists,* a group of scientifically minded philosophers inspired by Russell and Wittgenstein who emphasized the logical analysis of language.

Ryle was among the first thinkers at Oxford University to learn and apply the lessons of this new logic. Until his time, logic had been taught and studied at Oxford in the traditional fashion, without taking account of the new developments. But Oxford boasted a thriving tradition of work in the philosophy of mind, particularly in the area of sensory perception. In a nutshell, Ryle's originality lay in applying the logical techniques developed at Cambridge to some of the traditional philosophical problems studied at Oxford. Ryle's understanding of the complexities of these problems meant that his application was ultimately more influential than many earlier attempts to apply these techniques, by the logical positivists in particular.

Approach

Before Ryle wrote *The Concept of Mind*, he had discussed the idea of using the new ideas developed in the field of logic, Russell's in particular, to address traditional philosophical problems. Most famously, he put this idea forward in his 1932 paper "Systematically Misleading Expressions."[2] Ryle thought that many philosophical problems arise because features of our language mislead us. The solution is not to change our language, which serves us perfectly well in everyday life, but instead to beware of the confusions it leads us into.

Ryle also diagnoses the kind of mistake that he thought dualism arose from, referring to it as a "category mistake."* Such mistakes result from people putting things into the wrong logical category.* As an example, Ryle quotes a joke: "She came home in a flood of tears and a sedan chair." It works as a joke because she is not in a flood of tears in the same way that she is in a sedan chair (i.e. a chair in which a passenger is carried by pole-bearers): the tears and the chair belong to different categories, although the superficially similar grammar of the two expressions can hide this fact. Similarly, to say that someone is in a certain mental state is to refer to something that is in a different logical category from a physical state. You can have a memory just as you have a watch, for example, but it would be a mistake to look for the location of the memory the same way that you might search for the watch. Dualism, Ryle suggests, is based on confusing categories.

Contribution in Context

Ryle's book has many parallels with Ludwig Wittgenstein's *Philosophical Investigations*, a work that was largely completed at the time that Ryle was writing, even though it was not published until 1953, after Wittgenstein's death.[3] Ryle knew Wittgenstein, and he took part in many discussions with him and his followers. Wittgenstein's ideas were, therefore, familiar to him before they were published.

Like Ryle, Wittgenstein was concerned with coming to a philosophically satisfactory explanation of the relationship between mental states and behavior. And, like Ryle, he believed that this could not be achieved by seeing mental states as hidden states that could only be guessed at and not observed, and which were responsible for visible behavior.

Wittgenstein's and Ryle's ideas also run parallel to each other in their method. Neither man believed that philosophical problems could be resolved by constructing theories, in the way that scientific problems are. Instead, they felt that because such problems arose from confusions in our application of concepts, they should be resolved by what became known as "conceptual analysis"—that is, careful discussion of how concepts are used. Instead of asking what the mind is, philosophers should, they both felt, examine how the word "mind" is used, as well as the sort of context in which we find it necessary to refer to minds.

Along with British philosopher J. L. Austin,* Ryle is often considered to belong to a school called "ordinary language philosophy,"* although this is not a phrase that either of them used. Ordinary language philosophers accepted the logical positivist* emphasis on conceptual analysis, but thought that concepts were best analyzed by examining how words are used in everyday circumstances. They approached the study of concepts by looking first at the human context in which the concepts are employed.

NOTES

1 Gilbert Ryle, "Autobiographical," in *Ryle*, ed. Oscar P. Wood and George Pitcher (London: Macmillan, 1971), 12.

2 Gilbert Ryle, "Systematically Misleading Expressions," *Proceedings of the Aristotelian Society* 32 (1932).

3 Ludwig Wittgenstein, *Philosophical Investigations*, ed. G. E. M. Anscombe and R. Rhees, trans. G. E. M. Anscombe (Oxford: Blackwell, 1953).

SECTION 2
IDEAS

MODULE 5
MAIN IDEAS

KEY POINTS

- Ryle attacks dualism* as "the dogma of the ghost in the machine." He proposes that the mind is not an entity.

- Mental states are tendencies to behave in various ways.

- Ryle carefully analyzes the ways in which the concept* of mind and related concepts—like will, emotion, perception, and so on—are used.

Key Themes

Gilbert Ryle's main argument in *The Concept of Mind* has both negative and positive aspects. He is against dualist views of the mind, where human beings are believed to have two distinct parts, a body and a mind. Ryle argues that such views arise from a misunderstanding of what people think the mind is. Dualists make what Ryle calls a "category mistake."* That is, they confuse things that rightly belong to one category with another. They think of the mind as an entity like a body but separate from it and able to both affect it and *be affected by* it. Their view is that, compared with the human body, the human mind is "made up of a different sort of stuff and with a different sort of structure."[1]

Then Ryle offers his own, alternative view. The core of this view is the idea that many terms used to explain thought processes actually refer to dispositions, or tendencies towards something. To say that people are intelligent, or that they have a given belief, is to say that they are disposed to behave in certain ways. Ryle makes a strong conceptual connection between the mind and behavior.

" Such in outline is the official theory. I shall often speak of it, with deliberate abusiveness, as 'the dogma of the Ghost in the Machine.' I hope to prove that it is entirely false, and false not in detail but in principle. It is not merely an assemblage of particular mistakes. It is one big mistake and a mistake of a special kind. It is, namely, a category-mistake. **"**

Gilbert Ryle, *The Concept of Mind*

Also important to Ryle's argument is his view that practical knowledge* (knowledge of how to do something, like ride a bike—or "knowledge how") is distinct and different from theoretical knowledge* (knowledge of facts, such as that Paris is the capital of France—or "knowledge that"). I know how to ride a bicycle because when I want to ride one, I can do so. I have the necessary skills. This knowledge does not require knowledge of facts about how bicycles work.

Exploring the Ideas

For the dualist, because mental states are not physical causes of our behavior, they must therefore be non-physical causes. As a result, Ryle thinks that dualists assumed that there was a kind of hidden mechanism that was different to bodily mechanisms. These hidden mechanisms could not be observed or studied directly, though people would have first-hand knowledge of their own mechanisms.

Ryle thinks that this is the wrong conclusion to reach. When we say that people slam a door because they are angry, for example, what we mean is not that their anger is a hidden, non-physical cause of their behavior. Rather, what we mean is that they are disposed to act in an angry way. When we say that students did not come to class because they are lazy, we are drawing attention to the fact that this behavior fits an overall pattern.

Ryle writes that "when we describe people as exercising qualities of mind, we are not referring to occult episodes of which their overt acts and utterances are effects; we are referring to those overt acts and utterances themselves."[2]

So, for Ryle, words like "anger" and "laziness" refer not to hidden mechanisms, but to types of behavior that people are likely to exhibit. When we explain behavior by mentioning such things, we are not pointing to a *cause* of the behavior, we are making sense of it by showing that it fits a certain pattern.

The issue of practical knowledge illustrates Ryle's approach. What does it mean to say, "I know how to ride a bicycle"? According to what Ryle calls "intellectualism"*—the view that "knowledge how" is actually a form of "knowledge that"—it means that there is some knowledge inside me that I draw on when I ride the bicycle. Notice that this knowledge will be quite elaborate: it is very difficult for even a talented cyclist to describe how to ride a bicycle.

Intellectualism, Ryle argues, implies that to do anything intelligently, we must first think about some truth we know. To ride a bicycle well, we must think about the truths we know about how to ride bicycles. But contemplating a truth is itself something we can do either intelligently or unintelligently. To contemplate a truth, we must first know how to contemplate, which itself needs "knowledge how." That means at least some "knowledge how" must come before "knowledge that."

Ryle puts forward an alternative view. "Knowledge that" is best understood in terms of our tendency to behave in various ways. This should not be understood in too simple a fashion, though. You might know how to ride a bicycle without feeling liking riding one (for example, you might dislike cycling even though you are competent at it). But this ability must show itself in a disposition to behave in a certain way in certain circumstances: you could ride one if you had to; you could help a child to learn to ride a bicycle because you can do it, and so on. If there were no circumstances under which you would ride a bicycle, Ryle argues, then you do not count as knowing how to ride one.

Language and Expression

Ryle's argument is presented in a simple and informal style, and this has contributed to the book's popularity. The phrase "the ghost in the machine," which Ryle used to characterize the dualist view of the mind, was an effective slogan and is now a well-known phrase, lending itself, among other things, to the title of a 1967 nonfiction book by novelist Arthur Koestler and a 1981 album by the British rock band The Police. Ryle also writes with a great deal of humor, and his examples and illustrations display plenty of wit and imagination.

Ryle often refers to ordinary uses of mentalistic language—that is, language used to express thought processes: he mentions how people normally talk about intelligence, emotion, imagination, and so on. Recently, philosophers such as Timothy Williamson* have grown wary of Ryle's way of talking about ordinary language use in building his argument. They are suspicious of Ryle discussing what speakers of English or other natural languages would or would not say under various circumstances. According to him, for example, such speakers might not use a given word, not because it is *incorrect* to use it, but because it is impolite or unnecessary or irrelevant. The validity of such arguments has become a matter of controversy, throwing doubt on Ryle's methodology.

Ryle's book can be seen as controversial. He enjoys attacking the various mistakes and false views he thinks have supported the myth of the ghost in the machine. These include the view that mental states actually cause behavior, and that "knowledge-how" is a sort of "knowledge-that." In his introduction, Ryle says that he is not attacking such mistakes because he thinks they are foolish. In fact, he admits, they are mistakes he has made himself. "Primarily," he writes,

"I am trying to get some disorders out of my own system. Only secondarily do I hope to help other theorists to recognize our malady and to benefit from my medicine."[3]

NOTES

1   Gilbert Ryle, *The Concept of Mind* (London: Penguin, 2000), 20.

2   Ryle, *Concept of Mind*, 26.

3   Ryle, *Concept of Mind*, 11.

MODULE 6
SECONDARY IDEAS

KEY POINTS

- Ryle gives detailed accounts of specific mental states, including emotion, perception, and imagination.

- He also addresses our knowledge of our own mind. According to Ryle, we each learn about our own mind in much the same way as we learn about others' minds.

- Ryle's account of self-knowledge has been influential.

Other Ideas

Ryle spends much of *The Concept of Mind* applying his general theory of the mind to individual mental states. There are chapters on the will, emotion, perception, imagination, and so on, and Ryle illustrates how his theory that mental states are dispositions to behave in a certain way can shed light on each of these. In the course of doing so, he analyzes each mental subdomain. There are many interesting ideas in these detailed analyses. The chapter on the emotions, for example, is particularly rich because of the important distinctions Ryle draws between different sorts of emotion.

In chapter six, Ryle deals with the subject of knowledge of the mind. Part of the dualist* view that Ryle contests is the argument that there is a big difference between the ways I know my own mind and the ways I know other people's minds. According to this view, I can only observe other people's behavior, so I have to make inferences, or assumptions, from that behavior to create facts about their minds. In contrast, I have direct access to my own mind, which, in Ryle's words, has "Privileged Access to its own doings."[1]

❝ The sorts of things that I can find out about myself
are the same as the sorts of things that I can find out
about other people, and the methods of finding them
out are much the same. **❞**

Gilbert Ryle, *The Concept of Mind*

Ryle disagrees with both points of this dualist view: he argues that
people do not merely infer facts about others' minds from their
behavior, and, moreover, that people do not always know their own
mind directly. He discusses what he calls "avowals"—statements like "I
am bored." When I say this, I am not reporting something that I
already know; rather, I am expressing boredom. I can find out about
my own mental life by observing my avowals, just as I can learn about
other people's mental lives by observing theirs.

Exploring the Ideas

In his chapter on emotion, Ryle applies his general theory of the mind
to a particular case. According to the dualist viewpoint, emotions
occur in a person's consciousness and cause the person to act in some
way. For example, an emotion of anger is something that I can feel
inside me and that also causes me to slam the door. Likewise, an
emotion of love is something that I can feel inside me and that may
cause me to propose marriage.

Ryle argues that this view of emotion is mistaken. The word
"emotion," he says, has three important senses.[2] First, it can mean an
"inclination," which is a character trait. If people are vain, for example,
they are inclined to act vainly. Like other mental states, inclinations are
for Ryle dispositions to behave in various ways. They are not things a
person feels. Second, "emotion" can mean a mood, such as one of
melancholy. Again, to be in such a mood is to be inclined to act in
melancholy ways. Third, it can mean a feeling. A feeling is quite

different from an inclination or a mood. It is an occurrence that I notice inside myself, such as a twinge of anger. It does not motivate me to act in the same way that inclinations and moods do.

When he turns to discussing self-knowledge, Ryle is concerned with "avowals." In the dualist view, I know that someone else is bored by observing their behavior: I see the person yawn or fidget, or I hear them say, "I'm bored." But I know directly when *I* am bored by observing my own mind. When I say, "I'm bored," I am reporting occurrences in my own mind. But again, Ryle argues that this is a mistaken view. According to him, saying, "I am bored" is one of the things that boredom is a disposition to do. I can learn about my own moods by noticing my own behavior; this occurs when I surprise myself by blurting out expressions like "I am bored." It also occurs when I notice myself yawn or fidget. Thus, I find out about my own moods in essentially the same way that I find out about other people's moods.

"No metaphysical* Iron Curtain* exists compelling us to be for ever absolute strangers to one another," Ryle writes, adding, "no metaphysical looking-glass exists compelling us to be for ever completely disclosed and explained to ourselves."[3] What he means by this is that we are not always ignorant of other people's minds, and not only that, we do not always know our own minds.

Overlooked

In the final chapter, Ryle makes some interesting points about the nature of psychology, which has sometimes been defined as the science of the mind. But if Ryle is right and there is a deep conceptual connection between mind and behavior, there are other fields of study that could just as well be called sciences of the mind—for example, history, economics, and sociology. Each of these disciplines studies human behavior and uses a vocabulary of thought processes to describe it. History, for example, explains how people in the past behaved by referring to their opinions, motivations, and so on.

Psychology, unlike these other disciplines, could be seen as the study of the human mind itself and not of human behavior. Yet If Ryle is right in the overall thesis of his book, there is then no subject matter for psychology to study. After all, his main thesis is that mind and behavior are inextricably linked.

Ryle argues that psychology is not a "unitary inquiry."[4] It is not a counterpart to physics, for example, studying the laws that govern the mind in the same way that physics studies the laws that govern the external world. Instead, it is a mixture of loosely connected inquiries. Some psychologists study mental illness, for example, while others study the perceptual system. Just as medicine does not have a single clearly defined type of subject matter, neither does psychology.

In recent years, it has become more common to view the mind as a real internal structure possessed by human beings. This is because intellectuals such as Noam Chomsky* have argued that human behavior is so complex that we must propose a complex internal structure to explain it. As a result, psychology is sometimes viewed as the study of this structure. Ryle's alternative view of psychology is now seen as outdated by psychologists and philosophers, and is not widely accepted today.

NOTES

1   Gilbert Ryle, *The Concept of Mind* (London: Penguin 2000), 148.

2   Ryle, *Concept of Mind*, 110–11.

3   Ryle, *Concept of Mind*, 173.

4   Ryle, *Concept of Mind*, 305.

MODULE 7
ACHIEVEMENT

KEY POINTS

- *The Concept of the Mind* is widely regarded as a definitive attack on dualism.*

- Ryle's alternative theory of the mind was less influential, partly because of developments in psychology and linguistics.

- Ryle is often considered to be a notable advocate of behaviorism.*

Assessing the Argument

The Concept of Mind has both a positive and a negative purpose. Its negative purpose is to attack the dualist* picture of the mind—what Ryle calls "the dogma of the ghost in the machine," meaning the pervasive philosophical notion that the mind and the body are separate entities. Its positive purpose is to put forward an alternative view of mental states as dispositions to behave, or as tendencies towards certain behavior.

The book has certainly been more successful in achieving its negative purpose than it has in achieving its positive purpose. It is widely regarded by philosophers as a definitive attack on dualism, which has never come back into wide popularity. There are some contemporary philosophers, such as Frank Jackson* and Howard Robinson*, who defend forms of dualism, but they are a small minority.[1] Jackson and Robinson themselves have even influenced to some extent by Ryle's arguments. Contemporary dualists are typically property dualists* rather than substance dualists.* This means they argue not that the mind and the body are separate

> **"I come to bury logical behaviorism, not to praise it. "**
> Hilary Putnam, "Brains and Behavior"

things, but rather that mental and physical properties differ. Such dualism, they argue, is not vulnerable to Ryle's attack.

Although apart from Jackson, Robinson and a few others, most philosophers have largely agreed with Ryle in rejecting dualism, they have not accepted his alternative view. The consensus view is that Ryle ties mind and behavior too closely together. Linguist Noam Chomsky,* philosopher Jerry Fodor,* and others have argued that Ryle is too dismissive of the view that mental states are real internal structures of human beings that can cause behavior but that cannot be identified with it.

Achievement in Context

Ryle's views on the mind have fallen somewhat out of favor with philosophers since the 1950s and 1960s. They are associated to some degree with movements in mid-twentieth-century philosophy and psychology that have now become unfashionable—namely, logical positivism* and behaviorism.* These have become unpopular in part because of developments outside philosophy, in linguistics (the study of language), psychology, and computer science.

Logical positivism and behaviorism are connected with each other. According to logical positivists, statements are only meaningful if they can be properly tested. If mental states were hidden from observers, there could be no meaningful statements made about them. Logical positivists such as Rudolf Carnap* were drawn to behaviorism, the view that statements that are apparently about mental states could also, when analyzed, be about behavior.

This cluster of views was attacked with great success from the 1950s onwards by various writers, perhaps most significantly by the linguist Noam Chomsky. According to Chomsky, we can only explain human behavior by referring to the complex internal structures of human beings. For example, we cannot explain the ability of very young children to use complex language without advancing the idea of an internal knowledge of grammar.*

Chomsky himself has a more radical criticism of how Ryle framed the issue. Ryle wished to exorcise what he called "the ghost in the machine"—that is, he wanted to refute the idea that the mechanical brain, which could be investigated by natural science, was inhabited by a further entity, a mind, which should be investigated by psychology.

In contrast to this, Chomsky believes that the picture of a mechanical brain is a relic of old-fashioned science. As he has written, "Newton eliminated the problem of 'the ghost in the machine' by exorcising the machine; the ghost was unaffected."[2] For Chomsky, there is no reason to doubt the commonsensical idea that mental states are real and responsible for causing observable behavior. For him, such states should be investigated, like any other part of the natural world, by examining how they function, not by attempting to reduce them to brain states or anything else. In reality, the lines today between psychology and brain biology are blurred, and what was once thought of as the mind is studied in interdisciplinary centers where neuroscientists and psychologists focused on behavior work alongside each other.

Limitations

Outside philosophy, Gilbert Ryle's *The Concept of Mind* has had its greatest impact in psychology. It is frequently mentioned in psychological textbooks as a critique of dualism—the view that the body and the mind are distinct entities, and that a person is divided into these two entities. Ryle's attack on this idea—what he called the myth of the "ghost in the machine"—has made his work famous in philosophy, psychology, and beyond.

Psychologists also frequently describe Ryle's views as offering a model of behaviorism* concerning the mind. Behaviorism had been popular in early-twentieth-century psychology from a methodological point of view. Intellectuals thought that, since bodily behavior was all that could be observed and tested, if psychology were to qualify as a scientific form of study, it should restrict itself to that, leaving unobservable mental states out of consideration. Later, in the works of American psychologist B. F. Skinner,* behaviorism became a more philosophical approach: it was thought that mental states just *were* behavior. Academic psychologists often regard Ryle as a philosophical behaviorist of a more sophisticated kind than Skinner.

For example, in some psychological investigations, Ryle's discussion of emotions is sometimes mentioned as emphasizing the importance of behavior in attributing emotions to people. Ryle, though, did not regard himself as a behaviorist, and he would have been suspicious of some of the uses to which his ideas have been put in this literature.

NOTES

1   Frank Jackson, "Epiphenomenal Qualia," *Philosophical Quarterly* 32 (1982); Howard Robinson, *Matter and Sense* (Cambridge: Cambridge University Press, 1982).

2   Noam Chomsky, *New Horizons in the Study of Language and Mind* (New York: Cambridge University Press, 2000), 84.

MODULE 8
PLACE IN THE AUTHOR'S WORK

KEY POINTS

- Ryle felt that philosophical problems arose from a confusion about concepts,* so his work was devoted to clarifying concepts in different areas of thought.

- *The Concept of Mind* was Ryle's first book. It was written at the height of his career and is the major statement of his views.

- Ryle's reputation is based largely on *The Concept of Mind*—it is by far his most widely read work.

Positioning

The Concept of Mind was Ryle's first book, published when he was 49. But by that time Ryle was already a well-known philosopher. He had published many important articles, perhaps most significantly "Systematically Misleading Expressions,"[1] and in 1945 he had been appointed to the prestigious position of Waynflete Professor of Metaphysical Philosophy at Oxford University.

In many of his early articles, Ryle emphasized the importance of analysis of concepts and of language for the study of philosophy. He had put forward his view that philosophical problems come about because of confusion about concepts, arguing that the task of the philosopher was to clear up such confusion, rather than to discover new facts about the world, as scientists typically do.

In *The Concept of Mind*, Ryle applied his ideas about philosophical method to topics on the philosophy of mind. In particular, he used them to propose a new solution to the mind–body problem. Although Ryle's general views on method were already well known, *Concept* was his first major work on the mind.

> **❝** By the later 1940s it was time, I thought, to exhibit a sustained piece of analytical hatchet-work being directed upon some notorious and large-sized Gordian Knot.* After a long spell of methodological talk, what was needed now was an example of the method really working, in breadth and depth and where it was really needed. **❞**
>
> Gilbert Ryle, "Autobiographical"

Later in his life, Ryle returned several times to topics concerning the philosophy of mind, such as perception and the emotions. But he did not fundamentally change the position he argued for in *The Concept of Mind*, which represents the definitive statement of his views.

Integration

Throughout his career, Ryle thought of himself as describing "the logical geography of concepts."[2] He describes himself as trying to draw a map of our concepts to help us find our way about in them and to prevent confusion arising. *The Concept of Mind* is an example of this: in it, he tries to map out our concept of mind and other mental concepts, such as those of imagination, emotion, and will.

The shift in emphasis from building theories of the mind to providing analyses of our mental concepts reflects some of the lessons Ryle had learned from the logical positivist* philosophers in Vienna, and from Bertrand Russell* and Ludwig Wittgenstein* at Cambridge University. Philosophers had begun to regard their work as "conceptual analysis"—that is, as the study of words, concepts, and sentences in order to achieve a clarity of meaning. This way of understanding philosophy is reflected in the title *The Concept of Mind*. Philosophy was seen as being concerned with concepts—that is, ideas—and not with the physical world.

Ryle was concerned throughout his career with the metaphilosophical* questions of what philosophy is and what methods philosophers should use—metaphilosophy being the philosophical study of philosophy itself. *The Concept of Mind* applies to issues involved with the philosophy of mind—ideas about method that Ryle had developed and discussed throughout his career, starting with his widely read article "Systematically Misleading Expressions" in 1932, and culminating in a book-length treatment of the subject, *Dilemmas*, published in 1954.[3]

Ryle believed that philosophical problems arise because some expressions are "systematically misleading."[4] An example is the sentence "Mr. Pickwick is a fiction." The form of the sentence leads us to suppose that it is about Mr. Pickwick. But there is in fact no such person for the sentence to be about.

This theme concerned with the need to clarify concepts unifies Ryle's whole body of work. He wrote on the mind, on logic, on the philosophy of language, and on the ancient Greek philosopher Plato,* but in each case he was concerned with defining concepts clearly and with showing how philosophical problems arise from a failure to do so. This attitude goes hand in hand with a plain, unpretentious prose style—Ryle thought that inflated philosophical language was one of the causes of conceptual ambiguity.

Significance

Ryle was a dominant force in British philosophy in the 1940s and 1950s, but his reputation among philosophers has declined somewhat since. This is due in part to the decline of the philosophical movement he is generally associated with—that of "ordinary language philosophy."* It is often thought by philosophers today that ordinary language philosophers like Ryle and his colleague J. L. Austin* paid too much attention to how we talk and too little to what science can tell us about the world. According to this more recent view, there is too much in *The Concept of Mind* and Ryle's other works about the language we use to describe the mind, and too little about what psychology and neurophysiology (the branch of physiology dealing with the nervous system) have discovered about it—about the precise way in which the perceptual system works, for example.

The fact that Ryle's reputation has been sustained to the degree it has rests for the most part on *The Concept of Mind*, which is widely read among the general public and is a standard undergraduate text. Ryle also exerted a great deal of influence through his long teaching career at Oxford. Many of his students went on to become philosophers in their own right, and Ryle's influence can be traced through their work. But his other writings, especially those such as *Dilemmas* which were published after *The Concept of Mind*, are somewhat neglected today. A revival of interest in his work and a reassessment of its value may lie on the horizon.

NOTES

1   Gilbert Ryle, "Systematically Misleading Expressions," *Proceedings of the Aristotelian Society* 32 (1932).

2   Gilbert Ryle, *The Concept of Mind* (London: Penguin, 2000), 10.

3   Gilbert Ryle, *Dilemmas: The Tarner Lectures 1953* (Cambridge: Cambridge University Press, 1954).

4   Ryle, "Systematically Misleading Expressions."

SECTION 3
IMPACT

MODULE 9
THE FIRST RESPONSES

KEY POINTS

- Despite his own denials, Ryle was accused of being a behaviorist, and of not defining his notion of a "category mistake"* clearly enough.

- In response, Ryle pointed out that he, unlike the behaviorists, did not understand behavior purely in bodily terms.

- Ryle was already a well-known philosopher when *The Concept of Mind* was published, and it was widely read on publication.

Criticism

When Ryle published *The Concept of Mind* in 1949 he was already an established figure in the British philosophical scene. The book was read and studied by philosophers as soon as it came out, and its reception was mixed.

Early reviews by prominent philosophers, including Stuart Hampshire* in the philosophical journal *Mind*, and J. L. Austin* in the literary newspaper the *Times Literary Supplement*, praised the book.[1] But they and others also made serious criticisms. Both Hampshire and Austin wrote that the book was overly programmatic. Ryle did not fill in sufficient details of his own account of the mind. In criticizing dualism,* Ryle very reasonably gave alternative, non-dualist accounts of various aspects of the mental. But it is unclear how radical a thesis he intended to put forward: did he mean to claim that his book offered the correct way to approach the mind generally? Or was he just giving specific suggestions that showed how certain mental phenomena could be approached without lapsing into dualism?

❝ In short, what Ryle has succeeded in doing is to reduce the empire of the mind over a considerable area. This is an important achievement, and one that is brilliantly effected, but it does not fulfill Ryle's professed intention of entirely exorcising the ghost in the machine. The movements of the ghost have been curtailed but it still walks, and some of us are still haunted by it. **❞**

A. J. Ayer, "An Honest Ghost?"

Hampshire, for example, wrote that Ryle flips between two positions—one radical, the other modest. The radical thesis says that mental words stand not for invisible mental states, but rather for visible patterns of behavior. The modest thesis holds only that, in principle, we can investigate mental processes by observation: because what people do can be seen as relevant evidence for their states of mind, the minds of others are not unknowable.

Hampshire's point relates to a common strand running through much of the criticism Ryle's book received—namely, questioning whether Ryle was, despite his claims, a behaviorist.* Did he identify mental states with behavior? He seemed to analyze mental states in terms of dispositions or tendencies to behave, and to deny the existence of a private, inner life of the subject, a stream of consciousness, and so on. A. J. Ayer* argued that although Ryle seems to commit himself to behaviorism, at times he seems to fall back on the more modest thesis that, in applying mental concepts,* private, inner consciousness is less important, and overt behavior more important, than previous philosophers had supposed.[2]

A third critical point is more technical. Ryle depends on the notion of "logical categories."* He argued that we should not suppose that humans are blends of mind and body, because mind and body belong to different logical categories. However, critics such as J. J. C. Smart* complained that Ryle had not explained clearly enough what a logical category, and thus a category mistake,* is supposed to be.[3]

More broadly, Austin and others thought that Ryle had the mistaken idea that "logic"* was a tool that could on its own sort out puzzles about the mind—that is, that merely thinking about logic and logical categories could show us how to understand the relation between the mental and the physical.

Responses

Although Ryle remained philosophically active until his death in 1976, he rarely took part in debates with his critics. Yet he continued to modify and develop his position on the topics discussed in *The Concept of Mind*, and some of this later development shows the influence of the discussions that the work had led to.

In lectures in Oxford in 1964, Ryle addressed the issue of behaviorism—though not explicitly—when he discussed the concept of behavior.[4] At least in its more radical forms, behaviorism depends on a clear split between, on the one hand, supposed mental states and, on the other, purely physical behavior.

Ryle challenges this separation. He distinguishes instead between "mere bodily behavior" and "typically human behavior." The former is the sort of behavior that is also engaged in by animals. It can be described in purely physical terms. When it comes to typically human behavior, by contrast, we need mentalistic terms to describe it. We describe people as acting, for example, willingly or unwillingly, angrily or calmly. But while the radical behaviorist denies that such mentalistic terms are necessary to describe behavior, Ryle denies only that mental states—such as will, anger or calm—exist independently of behavior and can explain that behavior.

Conflict and Consensus

In later writings, Ryle developed his ideas about philosophical method, and specifically about the methods applied in *The Concept of Mind*. His next book, *Dilemmas*, published in 1954 and based on the 1953 Tarner Lectures at Cambridge University, sets out at length what amounts to a general theory of philosophy.[5] Different theories, he argues, addressing different problems and each apparently justified in its own right, appear to conflict in a way that is irreconcilable. Often, when we are faced with two apparently incompatible but well-justified theories, the problem is not that either one is wrong—rather, it is that the terms in which they are put lead to conceptual confusion. Philosophy's role is to sort out such confusion. Ryle developed this theory by referring to a range of philosophical topics, going far beyond the confines of the philosophy of mind.

In his article "Ordinary Language," Ryle argues that philosophy differs from science in that its proper study is our concepts, rather than the world.[6] But studying a concept is a matter of studying the way words are used, whether they are everyday words or technical terms used in the sciences. We grasp a word when we understand the rules or recipes for applying it correctly "in an unlimited variety of different settings."[7] Hence, Ryle claims, philosophers are justified in appealing to the ordinary usage of terms in the course of their investigations. This view is known today as "ordinary language philosophy."*

NOTES

1 Stuart Hampshire, "*The Concept of Mind* by Gilbert Ryle," *Mind* 59 (1950): 237–55; J. L. Austin, "Intelligent Behavior," *Times Literary Supplement*, April 7, 1950, xi.

2 A. J. Ayer, "An Honest Ghost?" in *Ryle*, ed. Oscar P. Wood and George Pitcher (London: Macmillan, 1971), 53–74.

3 J. J. C. Smart, "A Note on Categories," *British Journal for the Philosophy of Science* 4 (1953): 227–8.

4 Gilbert Ryle, *Aspects of Mind*, ed. René Meyer (Oxford: Blackwell, 1993).

5 Gilbert Ryle, *Dilemmas* (Cambridge: Cambridge University Press, 1954).

6 Gilbert Ryle, "Ordinary Language," *Philosophical Review* 62, no. 2 (1953): 167–86.

7 Ryle, "Ordinary Language," 179.

MODULE 10
THE EVOLVING DEBATE

KEY POINTS

- Many, if not most, philosophers of mind today are functionalists* who, like Ryle, hold that there is a fundamental connection between mental states and behavior. But, unlike Ryle, functionalists also believe that mental states are real internal states of human beings.

- Ryle's student Daniel Dennett* has influentially put forward the thesis that the mental and the physical are two ways of thinking and talking about human beings.

- Ryle also influenced thinkers such as Peter Hacker,* who believe that the job of philosophy is to map out our concepts—the categories we use to understand the world—and clarify connections between them.

Uses and Problems

In *The Concept of Mind*, Gilbert Ryle denies that mental states should be understood as complex internal structures of human beings that can explain behavior. His main target for attack is the dualist* view that these structures are non-physical. But he also denies that the mind can be identified with any physical structure.

In the decades since Ryle's book was published, it has become more common to argue that the mind *is* an internal physical structure, essentially the brain. This approach is assumed, for example, in much scientific work in psychology and linguistics. Psychologists see themselves as explaining behavior by reference to this structure. Philosophers such as David Armstrong* and David Lewis,* for example, hold that the mind and the brain are one and the same thing. They think that we can explain the causes of behavior by referring to states of the brain. Ryle's approach is seen by them as misguided.

> **❝** If philosophers have become very interested in language in the past fifty years it is not because they have become *dis*interested in the Great Questions of philosophy, but precisely because they *are* still interested in the Great Questions and because they have come to believe that language holds the key to resolve (or in some way satisfactorily dispose of) the Great Questions. **❞**
>
> Hilary Putnam, "Language and Philosophy"

However, one very common approach to the mind–body problem in philosophy of mind today, and indeed since the 1960s, does have some affinities with Ryle's view. This approach is *functionalism.**

According to functionalist thinkers such as Hilary Putnam,* mental states should not be identified either with physical states of the brain or with any non-physical states. Instead, mental states are functional states of the brain. Functions are defined in terms of input and output; if we see mental states in this way, it does not matter how they work, as long as they produce the right output given the right input. When we are angry, for example, our brain is in a state of the type caused by characteristic triggers of anger, which in turn causes us to engage in characteristically angry behavior.

The connection between functionalism and Ryle's view is that functionalism preserves a constitutive connection between mental states—such as anger—and behavior. That is, according to this view, mental states are not describable independently of the behavior they cause. Nevertheless, functionalism is not quite the same as Ryle's view. According to the functionalist, my anger on a particular occasion can be identified with some event in my brain at that moment, as long as that event was caused by characteristically anger-causing circumstances, and as long as it caused angry behavior on my part. Thus, to the functionalist, my anger is indeed an internal state of mine, which has a causal impact on my behavior.

Schools of Thought

There is no well-defined school in contemporary philosophy that follows Ryle's ideas and methods. But he has influenced some of today's scholars. His influence is clear, for example, in the school of thought that sprang from the later writings of Ludwig Wittgenstein.* Wittgenstein and Ryle knew each other, and their thought runs parallel in some important ways. They shared an idea of philosophy being geared toward the clearing up of conceptual confusion. Some of their specific views on the mind were also similar—for example, their emphasis on the importance of a person's behavior in being able to attribute a mental state to that person.

Some intellectuals who are primarily regarded as followers of Wittgenstein have drawn on Ryle's *The Concept of Mind* and other writings. For example, Peter Hacker,* who became prominent as an interpreter of Wittgenstein, appeals to some of Ryle's arguments against the common notion of the mind as an inner theater, where events occur that have causal impacts on the outside world but are themselves accessible only to the thinker him- or herself.

Hacker has also been influenced by Ryle's conception of philosophy. Like Ryle, he sees philosophers as mapping our concepts. He thinks that philosophy does not contribute new knowledge, as science does, but rather adds to our understanding of what we already know.[1]

In Current Scholarship

In several important respects, Ryle's philosophical program has been carried forward by his former student Daniel Dennett.* Dennett is well known for his notion of the "intentional stance," or "intentionality."* Intentionality means, roughly, "aboutness." Mental states—beliefs, desires, emotions— are typically *about* something. But the brain, as studied by neuroscience, does not display such "aboutness" in any obvious way. How, then, does intentionality fit into our scientific knowledge of the human mind?

Dennett gives a striking answer. Intentionality is *not* relevant to the sort of causal explanation that neuroscientists are interested in. Instead, we describe people in intentional terms when we want, for example, to predict their behavior. Under such circumstances, it becomes useful to adopt the intentional stance.[2] This approach sees the "causal-explanatory" and "intentional" ways of describing human beings as separate and non-competing. What that means is that human beings can be understood both as physical objects whose behavior is governed by physical causes, and as beings with minds whose behavior can be explained by reference to beliefs and desires. This approach is reminiscent of Ryle, despite its originality.

Ryle has also influenced Dennett in his methodology, in that Dennett considers philosophical problems to be conceptual rather than factual problems. For example, Dennett has written much about the issue of consciousness.[3] Philosophers and cognitive scientists often worry about how it is possible for consciousness to arise out of purely physical structures in the brain. Many of them suspect that some previously unknown mechanism must be at work, so they believe either that a new kind of science is necessary to answer the question, or that such a science is impossible and that the physical basis of consciousness will forever remain a mystery. Dennett, however, thinks that these conclusions are wrong: if such problems seem unsolvable, he argues, this shows that there is something wrong with the question, not that there is a good question without an answer.

A major difference between Dennett and Ryle, however, is that Dennett sees himself as focused on answering the same questions as scientists. He has often collaborated with scientists and thinks of philosophy and science as a joint enterprise trying to answer the same questions using, broadly, the same methods. In this, Dennett is arguably more typical of contemporary thought, which tends to regard science as a model for other disciplines.

NOTES

1   Peter Hacker, "Philosophy: A Contribution not to Human Knowledge but to Human Understanding," *Royal Institute of Philosophy Supplement* 65 (2009): 129–53.

2   Daniel Dennett, *The Intentional Stance* (Cambridge, MA: MIT Press, 1987).

3   See Daniel Dennett, *Consciousness Explained* (Boston: Little Brown, 1991).

MODULE 11
IMPACT AND INFLUENCE TODAY

KEY POINTS

- *The Concept of Mind* is still widely read but is considered less important by professional philosophers than it once was.

- Ryle challenges representationalism*—the dominant view in philosophy of mind suggesting that mental states function by representing the world.

- Representationalists have responded by arguing that mental states exist independently of behavior and explain it, and that practical knowledge ("knowledge how") should be understood as a way to represent facts.

Position

The Concept of Mind occupies a peculiar position in contemporary philosophy. It is widely read by the general public and is often recommended to undergraduate students of philosophy. Most professional philosophers are familiar with it, too. Yet Ryle's arguments are often ignored in contemporary discussions about the mind.

Partly, this is because Ryle's main target for attack is dualism* about the mind and the body. Dualism is no longer seen as a living opponent, so Ryle's argument against it has lost some of its relevance.

Still, Ryle's book provides several interesting and formidable challenges to contemporary thought. In particular, it provides a challenge to representationalism, which is perhaps the dominant view in philosophy of mind and cognitive science* today.

Ryle's method is also at odds with much of contemporary philosophy. Today, many philosophers, such as Jerry Fodor* and Timothy Williamson,* aim to study the mind in a factual, concrete

> **❝** It [*The Concept of Mind*] was a powerful and rhetorically winning attack, but not so many years later it was roundly and bluntly rejected by those philosophers and other theorists who saw the hope of a cognitive psychology, or more broadly a 'cognitive science,' a theory of the mind that was very close in spirit to the view Ryle was lampooning. **❞**
>
> Daniel Dennett, *The Intentional Stance*

way. They think that the problem of understanding mental states is not, after all, a conceptual problem but, rather, that it is an empirical* and scientific one. If philosophers wish to contribute to solving this problem, they should therefore collaborate with and learn from scientists. One way this belief manifests itself is in the idea that we can investigate mental states by investigating the brain. Ryle's emphasis on the analysis and clearing up of concepts rather than the building of theories challenges this approach.

Interaction

Representationalists hold that mental states, especially beliefs and desires, symbolize the world. Typically, they think that beliefs represent some way the world is, and that desires represent some way the world should be. These representations are encoded in the brain. In this way, they are genuine internal states of a subject: one's beliefs are, literally, inside one's head. We can appeal to them in explaining behavior, because brain states have a cause/effect relationship with the rest of the body.

If Ryle is right, this view misunderstands what mental states are. He argues that mental states—including beliefs and desires, but also perceptions, emotions, and moods—are not internal states of the subject that are responsible for causing the subject's behavior. For example, my belief that it is raining does not *cause* me to pick up an

61

umbrella. Rather, he argues, I can be said to believe that it is raining *because* I pick up the umbrella.

Ryle's challenge to the representational school of thought takes a more specific form in the second chapter of *The Concept of Mind*. There, he argues against the notion that practical knowledge* or "knowledge-how"—how to ride a bicycle, say, or to cook—is a form of "knowledge-that" or a knowledge of facts.

If Ryle is correct, then "knowledge-how" cannot be understood in terms of internal representations. It is more like a practical ability. Roughly speaking, he argues that people count as knowing how to cook only if, under certain circumstances, they can prepare a meal. Knowing how to cook is not a matter of an internal state of a person but rather is a matter of how they impact their environment.

But, Ryle thinks, "knowledge-how" is a crucial component of the mental. In particular, the notion of *intelligence* should be understood in terms of "knowledge-how," as should many related notions, such as those of being *logical* or *careful* or *stupid*. A whole range of central mental concepts,* such as intelligence and stupidity, are not representational.

The Continuing Debate

American philosopher Jerry Fodor,* a leading representationalist concerning the mind, offers a radical response to Ryle. We should embrace the disconnection between representations and behavior, he suggests. What is it, for example, to understand the word "computer"? Someone following Ryle might argue that we understand the word if we are able to use it in various ways—talk intelligently about computers, use the word "computer" correctly in a sentence, and so on. Fodor, however, thinks Ryle has it the wrong way round: we can do these things because we understand the word, and not vice versa.

Fodor also proposes explaining "knowledge-how" in terms of "knowledge-that." He argues that we should explain people's ability to participate in an activity in terms of their representational states; that is, we should explain my ability to ride a bicycle in terms of some representation encoded in my brain. The representation is like an explanation of how bicycles work: I am able to ride the bicycle because I have a sort of instruction manual in my mind, which tells me what to do.[1]

The same position is argued in an influential paper by Jason Stanley* and Timothy Williamson* that has sparked a great deal of debate in contemporary philosophy.[2] Stanley and Williamson's argument is complex, but in essence they suggest a way of understanding knowledge-how as a sort of knowledge-that. To know how to ride a bicycle, by their argument, is to possess knowledge of a particular kind of fact—one about how things work.

Ryle's strict distinction between science and philosophy has also been questioned. For example, David Armstrong* distances himself from Ryle in the beginning of his book *The Nature of Mind and Other Essays*.[3] Armstrong points to the growing realization among scientists that abstract theorizing forms an important part of the scientific method. Science is not just a matter of experiment and observation, but also requires theory. As a result, the boundary between science and philosophy has once again become blurred. Although they do not engage in experimental work, philosophers still have something to contribute to scientific study, in clarifying the concepts that scientists use to understand the world.

NOTES

1   Jerry Fodor, "The Appeal to Tacit Knowledge in Psychological Explanation," *Journal of Philosophy* 65 (1968): 627–40.

2   Jason Stanley and Timothy Williamson, "Knowing How," *Journal of Philosophy* 98 (2001): 411–44.

3   David Armstrong, *The Nature of Mind and Other Essays* (Brighton: Harvester, 1981).

MODULE 12
WHERE NEXT?

KEY POINTS

- There has been a recent renewal of interest in ordinary language philosophy,* and Ryle's work may be re-examined in this context.

- Anti-representationalism* about the mind has gained ground in recent years. Ryle is an important opponent of representationalism.

- *The Concept of Mind* is a well-written, accessible book that challenges many of our everyday assumptions about the mind. It is of enduring interest even if one finally disagrees with its conclusions.

Potential

The Concept of Mind is still widely read, but various aspects of the book make it less relevant today than it once was. One factor in this has been the dramatic decline in the popularity of behaviorism.* Ryle emphasizes behavior in his account of the various mental states, usually analyzing them as dispositions, or tendencies to behave in certain ways. But contemporary thinkers tend to identify mental states with physical structures or networks in the brain. Ryle's account seems outdated now.

Second, there has been a decline in the so-called ordinary language* school of philosophy with which Ryle is associated. Unlike Ryle, philosophers today generally see themselves as trying to understand the world just as much as scientists are. As a result, they tend to see philosophy and science as closely related, or even as two parts of a single activity.

66 *The Concept of Mind* is one of those books that is often cited by people who haven't read it but read about it, and think they know what is in it. They have read that it epitomizes two woefully regressive schools of thought that flourished unaccountably in mid-century but are now utterly discredited: Ordinary Language Philosophy and Behaviorism. Yes, and imbibing alcohol will inexorably lead you to the madhouse and masturbation will make you grow blind. Don't believe it. 99
Daniel Dennett, "Re-introducing *The Concept of Mind*"

Despite these factors, we can expect a revival of interest in the book. Dismissing Ryle as offering a standard behaviorist analysis of the mind is not really justified by the text. There is good reason to refer to Ryle as a behaviorist, but still his views are more subtle than the behaviorist label suggests.

There is also some evidence of a re-evaluation of ordinary language philosophy. Several contemporary philosophers, including Hilary Putnam,* Charles Travis,* and Avner Baz,* defend the tradition. Many of these thinkers have so far focused more on Ryle's Oxford University colleague J. L. Austin.* But a natural next step would be to take another look at Ryle, since Ryle and Austin were the two most eminent ordinary language philosophers.

Future Directions

The dominant theory in philosophy of mind today—one which stands opposed to Ryle's approach—is itself coming under attack. This theory is representationalism,* the view that mental states are representations of the world and are encoded in the brain. Representationalism suggests that our everyday talk of mental states—of beliefs, desires, emotions—tracks the brain's structure. Once we sufficiently understand the brain, we will be able to identify the structures to which these concepts* correspond.

Recently, an anti-representationalist critique has come about, inspired partly by discoveries in neuroscience about the structure of the brain.[1] According to this alternative view, the brain's structure differs from that of our mental concepts. For example, our thought and talk about the mind distinguishes beliefs from desires. But according to the anti-representationalist, there is no reason to suppose that a corresponding distinction will be found in the brain itself. This critique echoes Ryle, who felt that, although they were both valid, scientific, and commonsensical understandings of people were quite distinct from each other and not to be expected to correspond.

At the beginning of his career, Ryle was one of the few English-speaking philosophers to read and discuss the works of the phenomenological* school based in Germany, particularly those of Edmund Husserl* and Martin Heidegger.* This school of thought concentrated on the ways the world appears to individuals. Its authors are still largely unread in the philosophical tradition with which Ryle is associated, but Ryle acknowledged a debt to Husserl in particular. Some more recent philosophers—for example, the American Amie Thomasson*—have explored this intriguing connection, hoping to enrich analytical philosophy of mind with material from the continental tradition of thought about the mind.

Summary

The Concept of Mind is a memorable and compelling critique of dualism*—the view that the mind and the body are distinct entities, which somehow interact causally. This is a view that sometimes seems too old-fashioned to be worth criticizing, but Ryle argues convincingly that it has survived in various subtle forms in the way we think about the mind.

The book is also worthy of attention for the alternative account of the mind and of mental concepts* that Ryle advances. This aspect of *The Concept of Mind* is responsible for some of the neglect it has suffered in recent academic philosophy. Ryle's alternative to dualism has sometimes seemed out of date. In particular, his views come close to behaviorism, the currently unpopular view that says being in a particular mental state is a matter of behaving in certain ways—for example, to feel happy is to behave in ways that are characteristic of happiness.

But Ryle's views are more subtle than philosophers sometimes think. His analyses of mental concepts deserve re-evaluation: they are richer than some contemporary dismissals of them suggest. Ryle does not try to analyze or define talk about mental states in more basic, purely physical terms, as classical behaviorists did, but rather, he insists on the impossibility of such simplistic analyses. Some trends in recent philosophy suggest that interest in Ryle's work, along with that of his Oxford University colleague J. L. Austin, may be revived in the future.

The Concept of Mind is also well written. Ryle's style is engaging, often humorous, and the book is almost entirely free of technical terminology. In addition, Ryle is sparing with citations, footnotes, and other forbidding academic paraphernalia. As a result, the book has always been remarkably popular with the general reading public, far more so than most books written by academic philosophers.

NOTES

1   Tim van Gelder, "What Might Cognition Be, If Not Computation?" *Journal of Philosophy* 92 (1995): 345–81.

GLOSSARY

GLOSSARY OF TERMS

Behaviorism: the view that mental states should be understood in terms of overt behavior.

Behaviorists: people who hold that mental states are nothing more than behavior itself.

Category mistake: a mistake made when we confuse things of one category with things of another.

Cognitive science: the interdisciplinary study of the mind, encompassing parts of psychology, philosophy, linguistics, and computer science.

Concepts: concepts are usually understood in philosophy as general notions or ideas, or as the categories in terms of which we understand the world.

Dualism: the view that the mind and the body are distinct entities that jointly make up a human being.

Dualists: people who hold that the mind is an unobservable entity that lies behind and explains behavior.

Empiricism/Empirical approach: the idea that all knowledge should be gained by experience, by using experiments and observation to gather facts.

Functionalism: the view that mental states are functional states, to be identified by what they do. Fear, for example, is that state of a human being that is brought about by frightening experiences and that gives rise to fearful behavior.

Gordian Knot: an intractable problem; the term comes from a knot that, according to legend, could not be untied, and that was cut with a sword stroke by Alexander the Great.

Grammar: the study of the structural rules governing languages.

Intellectualism: the view that practical knowledge, or "knowledge-how," is a form of theoretical knowledge, or "knowledge-that."

Intentionality: the object-directedness or "aboutness" of a state. Fear is intentional, for example, insofar as it is fear *of* something.

Introspectionism: a psychological methodology that emphasizes psychologists' observation of their own mental states and processes.

Iron Curtain: a phrase popularized by Winston Churchill, referring to the post-war division between eastern and western Europe.

Linguistics: the study of human language.

Logic: a branch of mathematics and philosophy dealing with reasoning in general and inference in particular.

Logical behaviorism: the view that the meanings of terms about mental states come from behavior. The term "anger," for example, gets its meaning from angry behavior.

Logical categories: For Ryle, two things belong to different logical categories if replacing one for the other in a grammatically correct sentence results in absurdity. "Chair" and "table" belong to the same logical category, because the sentence "He made a chair and a table" is a sensible one. "Chair" and "a million dollars" belong to different logical categories, because the sentence "He made a chair and a million dollars" is absurd, though grammatically correct.

Logical positivism: a radical philosophical movement emphasizing the logical analysis of language. It was active from the late 1920s, especially in Austria and Germany.

Materialism: the view that human beings are purely physical or material beings. There is no non-material mind.

Mechanical philosophy: a view of the world that emerged in the seventeenth century, according to which nature is a mechanism. In this view, the behavior of things in nature is determined by the interaction of their microscopic parts.

Metaphilosophy: the philosophical study of philosophy itself.

Metaphysics: a branch of philosophy dealing with the ultimate or fundamental elements of reality, with what there fundamentally *is*.

Methodological behaviorism: a psychological methodology that emphasizes psychologists' observation of the outward behavior of subjects.

Ordinary language philosophy: a philosophical school associated with the University of Oxford that flourished in the 1950s and 1960s. It is characterized by careful attention to ordinary language.

Phenomenology: the study of the ways in which the world appears to individuals.

Practical knowledge: knowledge of how to do something—for example, knowledge of how to ride a bicycle or speak a language.

Property dualism: the view that things have two fundamentally different sorts of property, physical and mental.

Representationalism: the view that language and mind function primarily by representing the world accurately or inaccurately.

Substance dualism: the view that there are two different sorts of substance, mental and physical.

Theoretical knowledge: "knowledge-that," or knowledge of facts—for example, knowledge that Paris is the capital of France.

World War II: a major global conflict, involving most of the world's major powers, and lasting

PEOPLE MENTIONED IN THE TEXT

David Armstrong (1926–2014) was an Australian philosopher. He made seminal contributions both to the philosophy of mind and to metaphysics.

John L. Austin (1911–60) was a British philosopher and a leader of the so-called ordinary language school of philosophy. He made major contributions both to the philosophy of language and to the philosophy of perception.

A. J. Ayer (1910–89) was a British philosopher. He is perhaps best known for his book *Language, Truth and Logic* (1936), which introduced logical positivism to English-speaking audiences.

Avner Baz (b. 1964) is an Israeli philosopher. He is best known for his book that is a defense of ordinary language philosophy, *When Words are Called For* (2012).

Rudolf Carnap (1891–1970) was a German philosopher and the leader of the logical positivist* movement. He contributed to logic, the philosophy of language, and the philosophy of science.

Noam Chomsky (b. 1928) is an American linguist and political activist. His work on innate grammar has had a great influence on philosophy and psychology, as well as on linguistics.

Daniel Dennett (b. 1942) is an American philosopher. He has been an important contributor to the philosophy of mind in particular.

René Descartes (1596–1650) was a French scientist, mathematician, and philosopher. He is regarded as one of the most important philosophers of the modern era.

Jerry Fodor (b. 1935) is an American philosopher. He is best known for his contributions to the philosophy of mind and to cognitive science.

Pierre Gassendi (1592–1655) was a French scientist and philosopher. He wrote both on the theory of knowledge and on a wide range of scientific topics, making discoveries in astronomy and other fields.

Peter Hacker (b. 1939) is a British philosopher. He is one of the foremost interpreters of Ludwig Wittgenstein's work.

Stuart Hampshire (1914–2004) was a British philosopher. Often associated with the ordinary language school, he contributed to ethics, the philosophy of mind, and the history of philosophy.

Martin Heidegger (1889–1976) was a German philosopher. He is associated with the phenomenological school and is often considered to be one of the most important philosophers of the twentieth century.

Thomas Hobbes (1588–1679) was an English philosopher. He is best known for his work on political philosophy.

Edmund Husserl (1859–1938) was a German philosopher. He is considered to be the founder of phenomenology.*

Frank Jackson (b. 1943) is an Australian philosopher who is an Emeritus Professor at the Australian National University. His fields of interest are the philosophy of mind and metaphysics.

David Lewis (1941–2001) was an American philosopher. He contributed to many fields, including logic, the philosophy of language, metaphysics, and epistemology.

Nicolas Malebranche (1638–1715) was a French philosopher. He attempted to reconcile Christianity with the scientific worldview.

Plato (c. 428–348 BCE) was a seminal ancient Greek philosopher. He is frequently regarded as one of the greatest thinkers in history.

Hilary Putnam (b. 1926) is an American philosopher. He was an early proponent of functionalism, and has written widely on many areas of philosophy.

Howard Robinson (b. 1945) is University Professor of Philosophy at the Central European University in Hungary. His fields of interest are the philosophy of the mind and metaphysics, including the philosophy of religion.

Bertrand Russell (1872–1970) was a British philosopher, logician, social commentator, and political activist. His early work on logic and the foundations of mathematics helped to lay the foundations of analytical philosophy.

B. F. Skinner (1904–90) was an American psychologist. He developed a radical form of behaviorism* and applied it to the study of language.

J. J. C. Smart (1920–2012) was an Australian philosopher. He is perhaps best known for his materialist* view of the mind, according to which mental states are identical with states of the brain.

Jason Stanley (b. 1969) is an American philosopher. He has contributed to epistemology and to the philosophy of language.

Amie Thomasson (b. 1968) is an American philosopher. She has contributed to a number of fields, including metaphysics and the philosophy of art.

Charles Travis (b. 1943) is an American philosopher. He is noted for his contributions to the philosophy of language and the interpretation of Wittgenstein.

John B. Watson (1878–1958) was an American psychologist who was a professor of psychology at Johns Hopkins University. He is generally credited with founding the behaviorism school of psychology in his seminal 1913 article, "Psychology as the Behaviourist Views It."

Timothy Williamson (b. 1955) is a British philosopher working in the fields of epistemology, philosophical logic, and metaphysics.

Ludwig Wittgenstein (1889–1951) was an Austrian philosopher. He is widely regarded as one of the most important philosophers of the twentieth century.

Wilhelm Wundt (1832–1920) was a German psychologist who is considered to be the father of experimental psychology.

WORKS CITED

WORKS CITED

Armstrong, David. *The Nature of Mind and Other Essays*. Brighton: Harvester, 1981.

Austin, J. L. "Intelligent Behavior." *Times Literary Supplement*, April 7, 1950, xi.

Ayer, A. J. "An Honest Ghost?" In *Ryle*, edited by Oscar P. Wood and George Pitcher. London: Macmillan, 1971.

Broad, C. D. *The Mind and Its Place in Nature*. London: Kegan Paul, 1925.

Carnap, Rudolf. "Psychology in Physical Language." *Erkenntnis* 3 (1932/33): 107–42.

Chomsky, Noam. *New Horizons in the Study of Language and Mind*. New York: Cambridge University Press, 2000.

Dennett, Daniel. *The Intentional Stance*. Cambridge, MA: MIT Press, 1987.

Consciousness Explained. Boston: Little Brown, 1991.

"Re-introducing *The Concept of Mind*." *Electronic Journal of Analytic Philosophy* 7 (2002).

Descartes, René. *Meditations on First Philosophy*. Translated and edited by John Cottingham. Cambridge: Cambridge University Press, 1996.

Fodor, Jerry. "The Appeal to Tacit Knowledge in Psychological Explanation." *Journal of Philosophy* 65 (1968): 627–40.

Hacker, Peter. "Philosophy: A Contribution not to Human Knowledge but to Human Understanding." *Royal Institute of Philosophy Supplement* 65 (2009): 129–53.

Hampshire, Stuart. "*The Concept of Mind* by Gilbert Ryle." *Mind* 59 (1950): 237–55.

Jackson, Frank. "Epiphenomenal Qualia." *Philosophical Quarterly* 32 (1982): 127–36.

Putnam, Hilary. "Brains and Behavior." In *Analytical Philosophy: Second Series*, edited by Ronald J. Butler. Oxford: Blackwell, 1963.

"Language and Philosophy." In *Mind, Language and Reality*, edited by Hilary Putnam. Cambridge: Cambridge University Press, 1975.

Robinson, Howard. *Matter and Sense*. Cambridge: Cambridge University Press, 1982.

Ryle, Gilbert. "Systematically Misleading Expressions." *Proceedings of the Aristotelian Society* 32 (1932).

"Ordinary Language." *Philosophical Review* 62, no. 2 (1953): 167–86.

Dilemmas: The Tarner Lectures 1953. Cambridge: Cambridge University Press, 1954.

"Autobiographical." In *Ryle*, edited by Oscar P. Wood and George Pitcher. London: Macmillan, 1971.

Aspects of Mind. Edited by René Meyer. Oxford: Blackwell, 1993.

The Concept of Mind. London: Penguin, 2000.

Smart, J.J.C. "A Note on Categories." *British Journal for the Philosophy of Science* 4 (1953): 227–8.

Smith, Peter, and O. R. Jones. *Philosophy of Mind: An Introduction*. Cambridge: Cambridge University Press, 1986.

Stanley, Jason, and Timothy Williamson. "Knowing How." *Journal of Philosophy* 98 (2001): 411–44.

van Gelder, Tim. "What Might Cognition Be, If Not Computation?" *Journal of Philosophy* 92 (1995): 345–81.

Weitz, Morris. "Ryle's Logical Behaviorism." *Journal of Philosophy* 48 (1951): 297–301.

Wittgenstein, Ludwig. *Philosophical Investigations*. Edited by G. E. M. Anscombe and R. Rhees, translated by G. E. M. Anscombe. Oxford: Blackwell, 1953.

THE MACAT LIBRARY
BY DISCIPLINE

AFRICANA STUDIES

Chinua Achebe's *An Image of Africa: Racism in Conrad's Heart of Darkness*
W. E. B. Du Bois's *The Souls of Black Folk*
Zora Neale Huston's *Characteristics of Negro Expression*
Martin Luther King Jr's *Why We Can't Wait*
Toni Morrison's *Playing in the Dark: Whiteness in the American Literary Imagination*

ANTHROPOLOGY

Arjun Appadurai's *Modernity at Large: Cultural Dimensions of Globalisation*
Philippe Ariès's *Centuries of Childhood*
Franz Boas's *Race, Language and Culture*
Kim Chan & Renée Mauborgne's *Blue Ocean Strategy*
Jared Diamond's *Guns, Germs & Steel: the Fate of Human Societies*
Jared Diamond's *Collapse: How Societies Choose to Fail or Survive*
E. E. Evans-Pritchard's *Witchcraft, Oracles and Magic Among the Azande*
James Ferguson's *The Anti-Politics Machine*
Clifford Geertz's *The Interpretation of Cultures*
David Graeber's *Debt: the First 5000 Years*
Karen Ho's *Liquidated: An Ethnography of Wall Street*
Geert Hofstede's *Culture's Consequences: Comparing Values, Behaviors, Institutes and Organizations across Nations*
Claude Lévi-Strauss's *Structural Anthropology*
Jay Macleod's *Ain't No Makin' It: Aspirations and Attainment in a Low-Income Neighborhood*
Saba Mahmood's *The Politics of Piety: The Islamic Revival and the Feminist Subject*
Marcel Mauss's *The Gift*

BUSINESS

Jean Lave & Etienne Wenger's *Situated Learning*
Theodore Levitt's *Marketing Myopia*
Burton G. Malkiel's *A Random Walk Down Wall Street*
Douglas McGregor's *The Human Side of Enterprise*
Michael Porter's *Competitive Strategy: Creating and Sustaining Superior Performance*
John Kotter's *Leading Change*
C. K. Prahalad & Gary Hamel's *The Core Competence of the Corporation*

CRIMINOLOGY

Michelle Alexander's *The New Jim Crow: Mass Incarceration in the Age of Colorblindness*
Michael R. Gottfredson & Travis Hirschi's *A General Theory of Crime*
Richard Herrnstein & Charles A. Murray's *The Bell Curve: Intelligence and Class Structure in American Life*
Elizabeth Loftus's *Eyewitness Testimony*
Jay Macleod's *Ain't No Makin' It: Aspirations and Attainment in a Low-Income Neighborhood*
Philip Zimbardo's *The Lucifer Effect*

ECONOMICS

Janet Abu-Lughod's *Before European Hegemony*
Ha-Joon Chang's *Kicking Away the Ladder*
David Brion Davis's *The Problem of Slavery in the Age of Revolution*
Milton Friedman's *The Role of Monetary Policy*
Milton Friedman's *Capitalism and Freedom*
David Graeber's *Debt: the First 5000 Years*
Friedrich Hayek's *The Road to Serfdom*
Karen Ho's *Liquidated: An Ethnography of Wall Street*

The Macat Library By Discipline

John Maynard Keynes's *The General Theory of Employment, Interest and Money*
Charles P. Kindleberger's *Manias, Panics and Crashes*
Robert Lucas's *Why Doesn't Capital Flow from Rich to Poor Countries?*
Burton G. Malkiel's *A Random Walk Down Wall Street*
Thomas Robert Malthus's *An Essay on the Principle of Population*
Karl Marx's *Capital*
Thomas Piketty's *Capital in the Twenty-First Century*
Amartya Sen's *Development as Freedom*
Adam Smith's *The Wealth of Nations*
Nassim Nicholas Taleb's *The Black Swan: The Impact of the Highly Improbable*
Amos Tversky's & Daniel Kahneman's *Judgment under Uncertainty: Heuristics and Biases*
Mahbub Ul Haq's *Reflections on Human Development*
Max Weber's *The Protestant Ethic and the Spirit of Capitalism*

FEMINISM AND GENDER STUDIES

Judith Butler's *Gender Trouble*
Simone De Beauvoir's *The Second Sex*
Michel Foucault's *History of Sexuality*
Betty Friedan's *The Feminine Mystique*
Saba Mahmood's *The Politics of Piety: The Islamic Revival and the Feminist Subject*
Joan Wallach Scott's *Gender and the Politics of History*
Mary Wollstonecraft's *A Vindication of the Rights of Woman*
Virginia Woolf's *A Room of One's Own*

GEOGRAPHY

The Brundtland Report's *Our Common Future*
Rachel Carson's *Silent Spring*
Charles Darwin's *On the Origin of Species*
James Ferguson's *The Anti-Politics Machine*
Jane Jacobs's *The Death and Life of Great American Cities*
James Lovelock's *Gaia: A New Look at Life on Earth*
Amartya Sen's *Development as Freedom*
Mathis Wackernagel & William Rees's *Our Ecological Footprint*

HISTORY

Janet Abu-Lughod's *Before European Hegemony*
Benedict Anderson's *Imagined Communities*
Bernard Bailyn's *The Ideological Origins of the American Revolution*
Hanna Batatu's *The Old Social Classes And The Revolutionary Movements Of Iraq*
Christopher Browning's *Ordinary Men: Reserve Police Batallion 101 and the Final Solution in Poland*
Edmund Burke's *Reflections on the Revolution in France*
William Cronon's *Nature's Metropolis: Chicago And The Great West*
Alfred W. Crosby's *The Columbian Exchange*
Hamid Dabashi's *Iran: A People Interrupted*
David Brion Davis's *The Problem of Slavery in the Age of Revolution*
Nathalie Zemon Davis's *The Return of Martin Guerre*
Jared Diamond's *Guns, Germs & Steel: the Fate of Human Societies*
Frank Dikotter's *Mao's Great Famine*
John W Dower's *War Without Mercy: Race And Power In The Pacific War*
W. E. B. Du Bois's *The Souls of Black Folk*
Richard J. Evans's *In Defence of History*
Lucien Febvre's *The Problem of Unbelief in the 16th Century*
Sheila Fitzpatrick's *Everyday Stalinism*

Eric Foner's *Reconstruction: America's Unfinished Revolution, 1863-1877*
Michel Foucault's *Discipline and Punish*
Michel Foucault's *History of Sexuality*
Francis Fukuyama's *The End of History and the Last Man*
John Lewis Gaddis's *We Now Know: Rethinking Cold War History*
Ernest Gellner's *Nations and Nationalism*
Eugene Genovese's *Roll, Jordan, Roll: The World the Slaves Made*
Carlo Ginzburg's *The Night Battles*
Daniel Goldhagen's *Hitler's Willing Executioners*
Jack Goldstone's *Revolution and Rebellion in the Early Modern World*
Antonio Gramsci's *The Prison Notebooks*
Alexander Hamilton, John Jay & James Madison's *The Federalist Papers*
Christopher Hill's *The World Turned Upside Down*
Carole Hillenbrand's *The Crusades: Islamic Perspectives*
Thomas Hobbes's *Leviathan*
Eric Hobsbawm's *The Age Of Revolution*
John A. Hobson's *Imperialism: A Study*
Albert Hourani's *History of the Arab Peoples*
Samuel P. Huntington's *The Clash of Civilizations and the Remaking of World Order*
C. L. R. James's *The Black Jacobins*
Tony Judt's *Postwar: A History of Europe Since 1945*
Ernst Kantorowicz's *The King's Two Bodies: A Study in Medieval Political Theology*
Paul Kennedy's *The Rise and Fall of the Great Powers*
Ian Kershaw's *The "Hitler Myth": Image and Reality in the Third Reich*
John Maynard Keynes's *The General Theory of Employment, Interest and Money*
Charles P. Kindleberger's *Manias, Panics and Crashes*
Martin Luther King Jr's *Why We Can't Wait*
Henry Kissinger's *World Order: Reflections on the Character of Nations and the Course of History*
Thomas Kuhn's *The Structure of Scientific Revolutions*
Georges Lefebvre's *The Coming of the French Revolution*
John Locke's *Two Treatises of Government*
Niccolò Machiavelli's *The Prince*
Thomas Robert Malthus's *An Essay on the Principle of Population*
Mahmood Mamdani's *Citizen and Subject: Contemporary Africa And The Legacy Of Late Colonialism*
Karl Marx's *Capital*
Stanley Milgram's *Obedience to Authority*
John Stuart Mill's *On Liberty*
Thomas Paine's *Common Sense*
Thomas Paine's *Rights of Man*
Geoffrey Parker's *Global Crisis: War, Climate Change and Catastrophe in the Seventeenth Century*
Jonathan Riley-Smith's *The First Crusade and the Idea of Crusading*
Jean-Jacques Rousseau's *The Social Contract*
Joan Wallach Scott's *Gender and the Politics of History*
Theda Skocpol's *States and Social Revolutions*
Adam Smith's *The Wealth of Nations*
Timothy Snyder's *Bloodlands: Europe Between Hitler and Stalin*
Sun Tzu's *The Art of War*
Keith Thomas's *Religion and the Decline of Magic*
Thucydides's *The History of the Peloponnesian War*
Frederick Jackson Turner's *The Significance of the Frontier in American History*
Odd Arne Westad's *The Global Cold War: Third World Interventions And The Making Of Our Times*

LITERATURE

Chinua Achebe's *An Image of Africa: Racism in Conrad's Heart of Darkness*
Roland Barthes's *Mythologies*
Homi K. Bhabha's *The Location of Culture*
Judith Butler's *Gender Trouble*
Simone De Beauvoir's *The Second Sex*
Ferdinand De Saussure's *Course in General Linguistics*
T. S. Eliot's *The Sacred Wood: Essays on Poetry and Criticism*
Zora Neale Huston's *Characteristics of Negro Expression*
Toni Morrison's *Playing in the Dark: Whiteness in the American Literary Imagination*
Edward Said's *Orientalism*
Gayatri Chakravorty Spivak's *Can the Subaltern Speak?*
Mary Wollstonecraft's *A Vindication of the Rights of Women*
Virginia Woolf's *A Room of One's Own*

PHILOSOPHY

Elizabeth Anscombe's *Modern Moral Philosophy*
Hannah Arendt's *The Human Condition*
Aristotle's *Metaphysics*
Aristotle's *Nicomachean Ethics*
Edmund Gettier's *Is Justified True Belief Knowledge?*
Georg Wilhelm Friedrich Hegel's *Phenomenology of Spirit*
David Hume's *Dialogues Concerning Natural Religion*
David Hume's *The Enquiry for Human Understanding*
Immanuel Kant's *Religion within the Boundaries of Mere Reason*
Immanuel Kant's *Critique of Pure Reason*
Søren Kierkegaard's *The Sickness Unto Death*
Søren Kierkegaard's *Fear and Trembling*
C. S. Lewis's *The Abolition of Man*
Alasdair MacIntyre's *After Virtue*
Marcus Aurelius's *Meditations*
Friedrich Nietzsche's *On the Genealogy of Morality*
Friedrich Nietzsche's *Beyond Good and Evil*
Plato's *Republic*
Plato's *Symposium*
Jean-Jacques Rousseau's *The Social Contract*
Gilbert Ryle's *The Concept of Mind*
Baruch Spinoza's *Ethics*
Sun Tzu's *The Art of War*
Ludwig Wittgenstein's *Philosophical Investigations*

POLITICS

Benedict Anderson's *Imagined Communities*
Aristotle's *Politics*
Bernard Bailyn's *The Ideological Origins of the American Revolution*
Edmund Burke's *Reflections on the Revolution in France*
John C. Calhoun's *A Disquisition on Government*
Ha-Joon Chang's *Kicking Away the Ladder*
Hamid Dabashi's *Iran: A People Interrupted*
Hamid Dabashi's *Theology of Discontent: The Ideological Foundation of the Islamic Revolution in Iran*
Robert Dahl's *Democracy and its Critics*
Robert Dahl's *Who Governs?*
David Brion Davis's *The Problem of Slavery in the Age of Revolution*

Alexis De Tocqueville's *Democracy in America*
James Ferguson's *The Anti-Politics Machine*
Frank Dikotter's *Mao's Great Famine*
Sheila Fitzpatrick's *Everyday Stalinism*
Eric Foner's *Reconstruction: America's Unfinished Revolution, 1863-1877*
Milton Friedman's *Capitalism and Freedom*
Francis Fukuyama's *The End of History and the Last Man*
John Lewis Gaddis's *We Now Know: Rethinking Cold War History*
Ernest Gellner's *Nations and Nationalism*
David Graeber's *Debt: the First 5000 Years*
Antonio Gramsci's *The Prison Notebooks*
Alexander Hamilton, John Jay & James Madison's *The Federalist Papers*
Friedrich Hayek's *The Road to Serfdom*
Christopher Hill's *The World Turned Upside Down*
Thomas Hobbes's *Leviathan*
John A. Hobson's *Imperialism: A Study*
Samuel P. Huntington's *The Clash of Civilizations and the Remaking of World Order*
Tony Judt's *Postwar: A History of Europe Since 1945*
David C. Kang's *China Rising: Peace, Power and Order in East Asia*
Paul Kennedy's *The Rise and Fall of Great Powers*
Robert Keohane's *After Hegemony*
Martin Luther King Jr.'s *Why We Can't Wait*
Henry Kissinger's *World Order: Reflections on the Character of Nations and the Course of History*
John Locke's *Two Treatises of Government*
Niccolò Machiavelli's *The Prince*
Thomas Robert Malthus's *An Essay on the Principle of Population*
Mahmood Mamdani's *Citizen and Subject: Contemporary Africa And The Legacy Of Late Colonialism*
Karl Marx's *Capital*
John Stuart Mill's *On Liberty*
John Stuart Mill's *Utilitarianism*
Hans Morgenthau's *Politics Among Nations*
Thomas Paine's *Common Sense*
Thomas Paine's *Rights of Man*
Thomas Piketty's *Capital in the Twenty-First Century*
Robert D. Putman's *Bowling Alone*
John Rawls's *Theory of Justice*
Jean-Jacques Rousseau's *The Social Contract*
Theda Skocpol's *States and Social Revolutions*
Adam Smith's *The Wealth of Nations*
Sun Tzu's *The Art of War*
Henry David Thoreau's *Civil Disobedience*
Thucydides's *The History of the Peloponnesian War*
Kenneth Waltz's *Theory of International Politics*
Max Weber's *Politics as a Vocation*
Odd Arne Westad's *The Global Cold War: Third World Interventions And The Making Of Our Times*

POSTCOLONIAL STUDIES

Roland Barthes's *Mythologies*
Frantz Fanon's *Black Skin, White Masks*
Homi K. Bhabha's *The Location of Culture*
Gustavo Gutiérrez's *A Theology of Liberation*
Edward Said's *Orientalism*
Gayatri Chakravorty Spivak's *Can the Subaltern Speak?*

The Macat Library By Discipline

PSYCHOLOGY

Gordon Allport's *The Nature of Prejudice*
Alan Baddeley & Graham Hitch's *Aggression: A Social Learning Analysis*
Albert Bandura's *Aggression: A Social Learning Analysis*
Leon Festinger's *A Theory of Cognitive Dissonance*
Sigmund Freud's *The Interpretation of Dreams*
Betty Friedan's *The Feminine Mystique*
Michael R. Gottfredson & Travis Hirschi's *A General Theory of Crime*
Eric Hoffer's *The True Believer: Thoughts on the Nature of Mass Movements*
William James's *Principles of Psychology*
Elizabeth Loftus's *Eyewitness Testimony*
A. H. Maslow's *A Theory of Human Motivation*
Stanley Milgram's *Obedience to Authority*
Steven Pinker's *The Better Angels of Our Nature*
Oliver Sacks's *The Man Who Mistook His Wife For a Hat*
Richard Thaler & Cass Sunstein's *Nudge: Improving Decisions About Health, Wealth and Happiness*
Amos Tversky's *Judgment under Uncertainty: Heuristics and Biases*
Philip Zimbardo's *The Lucifer Effect*

SCIENCE

Rachel Carson's *Silent Spring*
William Cronon's *Nature's Metropolis: Chicago And The Great West*
Alfred W. Crosby's *The Columbian Exchange*
Charles Darwin's *On the Origin of Species*
Richard Dawkin's *The Selfish Gene*
Thomas Kuhn's *The Structure of Scientific Revolutions*
Geoffrey Parker's *Global Crisis: War, Climate Change and Catastrophe in the Seventeenth Century*
Mathis Wackernagel & William Rees's *Our Ecological Footprint*

SOCIOLOGY

Michelle Alexander's *The New Jim Crow: Mass Incarceration in the Age of Colorblindness*
Gordon Allport's *The Nature of Prejudice*
Albert Bandura's *Aggression: A Social Learning Analysis*
Hanna Batatu's *The Old Social Classes And The Revolutionary Movements Of Iraq*
Ha-Joon Chang's *Kicking Away the Ladder*
W. E. B. Du Bois's *The Souls of Black Folk*
Émile Durkheim's *On Suicide*
Frantz Fanon's *Black Skin, White Masks*
Frantz Fanon's *The Wretched of the Earth*
Eric Foner's *Reconstruction: America's Unfinished Revolution, 1863-1877*
Eugene Genovese's *Roll, Jordan, Roll: The World the Slaves Made*
Jack Goldstone's *Revolution and Rebellion in the Early Modern World*
Antonio Gramsci's *The Prison Notebooks*
Richard Herrnstein & Charles A Murray's *The Bell Curve: Intelligence and Class Structure in American Life*
Eric Hoffer's *The True Believer: Thoughts on the Nature of Mass Movements*
Jane Jacobs's *The Death and Life of Great American Cities*
Robert Lucas's *Why Doesn't Capital Flow from Rich to Poor Countries?*
Jay Macleod's *Ain't No Makin' It: Aspirations and Attainment in a Low Income Neighborhood*
Elaine May's *Homeward Bound: American Families in the Cold War Era*
Douglas McGregor's *The Human Side of Enterprise*
C. Wright Mills's *The Sociological Imagination*

Thomas Piketty's *Capital in the Twenty-First Century*
Robert D. Putman's *Bowling Alone*
David Riesman's *The Lonely Crowd: A Study of the Changing American Character*
Edward Said's *Orientalism*
Joan Wallach Scott's *Gender and the Politics of History*
Theda Skocpol's *States and Social Revolutions*
Max Weber's *The Protestant Ethic and the Spirit of Capitalism*

THEOLOGY

Augustine's *Confessions*
Benedict's *Rule of St Benedict*
Gustavo Gutiérrez's *A Theology of Liberation*
Carole Hillenbrand's *The Crusades: Islamic Perspectives*
David Hume's *Dialogues Concerning Natural Religion*
Immanuel Kant's *Religion within the Boundaries of Mere Reason*
Ernst Kantorowicz's *The King's Two Bodies: A Study in Medieval Political Theology*
Søren Kierkegaard's *The Sickness Unto Death*
C. S. Lewis's *The Abolition of Man*
Saba Mahmood's *The Politics of Piety: The Islamic Revival and the Feminist Subject*
Baruch Spinoza's *Ethics*
Keith Thomas's *Religion and the Decline of Magic*

COMING SOON

Chris Argyris's *The Individual and the Organisation*
Seyla Benhabib's *The Rights of Others*
Walter Benjamin's *The Work Of Art in the Age of Mechanical Reproduction*
John Berger's *Ways of Seeing*
Pierre Bourdieu's *Outline of a Theory of Practice*
Mary Douglas's *Purity and Danger*
Roland Dworkin's *Taking Rights Seriously*
James G. March's *Exploration and Exploitation in Organisational Learning*
Ikujiro Nonaka's *A Dynamic Theory of Organizational Knowledge Creation*
Griselda Pollock's *Vision and Difference*
Amartya Sen's *Inequality Re-Examined*
Susan Sontag's *On Photography*
Yasser Tabbaa's *The Transformation of Islamic Art*
Ludwig von Mises's *Theory of Money and Credit*

Macat Disciplines

Access the greatest ideas and thinkers across entire disciplines, including

GLOBALIZATION

Arjun Appadurai's, *Modernity at Large: Cultural Dimensions of Globalisation*

James Ferguson's, *The Anti-Politics Machine*

Geert Hofstede's, *Culture's Consequences*

Amartya Sen's, *Development as Freedom*

Macat Pairs

Analyse historical and modern issues from opposite sides of an argument. Pairs include:

HOW TO RUN AN ECONOMY

John Maynard Keynes's
The General Theory OF Employment, Interest and Money

Classical economics suggests that market economies are self-correcting in times of recession or depression, and tend toward full employment and output. But English economist John Maynard Keynes disagrees.

In his ground-breaking 1936 study *The General Theory*, Keynes argues that traditional economics has misunderstood the causes of unemployment. Employment is not determined by the price of labor; it is directly linked to demand. Keynes believes market economies are by nature unstable, and so require government intervention. Spurred on by the social catastrophe of the Great Depression of the 1930s, he sets out to revolutionize the way the world thinks

Milton Friedman's
The Role of Monetary Policy

Friedman's 1968 paper changed the course of economic theory. In just 17 pages, he demolished existing theory and outlined an effective alternate monetary policy designed to secure 'high employment, stable prices and rapid growth.'

Friedman demonstrated that monetary policy plays a vital role in broader economic stability and argued that economists got their monetary policy wrong in the 1950s and 1960s by misunderstanding the relationship between inflation and unemployment. Previous generations of economists had believed that governments could permanently decrease unemployment by permitting inflation—and vice versa. Friedman's most original contribution was to show that this supposed trade-off is an illusion that only works in the short term.

Macat analyses are available from all good bookshops and libraries.

Access hundreds of analyses through one, multimedia tool.
Join free for one month **library.macat.com**

Macat Disciplines

Access the greatest ideas and thinkers across entire disciplines, including

THE FUTURE OF DEMOCRACY

Robert A. Dahl's, *Democracy and Its Critics*
Robert A. Dahl's, *Who Governs?*
Alexis De Toqueville's, *Democracy in America*
Niccolò Machiavelli's, *The Prince*
John Stuart Mill's, *On Liberty*
Robert D. Putnam's, *Bowling Alone*
Jean-Jacques Rousseau's, *The Social Contract*
Henry David Thoreau's, *Civil Disobedience*

Macat Disciplines

Access the greatest ideas and thinkers across entire disciplines, including

TOTALITARIANISM

Sheila Fitzpatrick's, *Everyday Stalinism*
Ian Kershaw's, *The "Hitler Myth"*
Timothy Snyder's, *Bloodlands*

Macat Pairs

Analyse historical and modern issues from opposite sides of an argument. Pairs include:

RACE AND IDENTITY

Zora Neale Hurston's
Characteristics of Negro Expression

Using material collected on anthropological expeditions to the South, Zora Neale Hurston explains how expression in African American culture in the early twentieth century departs from the art of white America. At the time, African American art was often criticized for copying white culture. For Hurston, this criticism misunderstood how art works. European tradition views art as something fixed. But Hurston describes a creative process that is alive, ever-changing, and largely improvisational. She maintains that African American art works through a process called 'mimicry'—where an imitated object or verbal pattern, for example, is reshaped and altered until it becomes something new, novel—and worthy of attention.

Frantz Fanon's
Black Skin, White Masks

Black Skin, White Masks offers a radical analysis of the psychological effects of colonization on the colonized.

Fanon witnessed the effects of colonization first hand both in his birthplace, Martinique, and again later in life when he worked as a psychiatrist in another French colony, Algeria. His text is uncompromising in form and argument. He dissects the dehumanizing effects of colonialism, arguing that it destroys the native sense of identity, forcing people to adapt to an alien set of values—including a core belief that they are inferior. This results in deep psychological trauma.

Fanon's work played a pivotal role in the civil rights movements of the 1960s.

Macat analyses are available from all good bookshops and libraries.

Access hundreds of analyses through one, multimedia tool.
Join free for one month **library.macat.com**

Macat Pairs

Analyse historical and modern issues from opposite sides of an argument. Pairs include:

INTERNATIONAL RELATIONS IN THE 21ST CENTURY

Samuel P. Huntington's
The Clash of Civilisations

In his highly influential 1996 book, Huntington offers a vision of a post-Cold War world in which conflict takes place not between competing ideologies but between cultures. The worst clash, he argues, will be between the Islamic world and the West: the West's arrogance and belief that its culture is a "gift" to the world will come into conflict with Islam's obstinacy and concern that its culture is under attack from a morally decadent "other."

Clash inspired much debate between different political schools of thought. But its greatest impact came in helping define American foreign policy in the wake of the 2001 terrorist attacks in New York and Washington.

Francis Fukuyama's
The End of History and the Last Man

Published in 1992, *The End of History and the Last Man* argues that capitalist democracy is the final destination for all societies. Fukuyama believed democracy triumphed during the Cold War because it lacks the "fundamental contradictions" inherent in communism and satisfies our yearning for freedom and equality. Democracy therefore marks the endpoint in the evolution of ideology, and so the "end of history." There will still be "events," but no fundamental change in ideology.

Macat Disciplines

Access the greatest ideas and thinkers across entire disciplines, including

MAN AND THE ENVIRONMENT

The Brundtland Report's, *Our Common Future*
Rachel Carson's, *Silent Spring*
James Lovelock's, *Gaia: A New Look at Life on Earth*
Mathis Wackernagel & William Rees's, *Our Ecological Footprint*

Macat analyses are available from all good bookshops and libraries.

Access hundreds of analyses through one, multimedia tool.
Join free for one month **library.macat.com**

For Product Safety Concerns and Information please contact our EU
representative GPSR@taylorandfrancis.com Taylor & Francis Verlag GmbH,
Kaufingerstraße 24, 80331 München, Germany

Printed and bound by CPI Group (UK) Ltd, Croydon, CR0 4YY
08/06/2025
01896998-0002